THE RAW CONFE

GOOD
GIRL

FOREWORD BY LYNSI SNYDER
OWNER & PRESIDENT OF IN-N-OUT BURGER

VICTORIA RAE RICH

outskirts
press

About the Author

by the Good Girl Gang

"Victoria Rich is extremely bold and brave! She travels the world evangelizing with her nonprofit, CRAVE the Movement, and she literally risked her life to be the first woman in thousands of years to legally preach The Gospel of Jesus in Egypt (It doesn't get much more legit than that!) In addition to being a gifted preacher, she is also a phenomenal singer and worship leader. Victoria is one of the most loving, giving, and anointed people on the planet!"
  • Brianna Kendrick of Minneapolis, MN

"Victoria is the type of friend and mentor every parent would want their kids to have! She's full of life, love, passion, zeal and God's truth. She is one of the bravest, boldest, wildest and authentic Kingdom warriors I know!"
  • Tausha Prince of Seattle, WA

"Tori is incredibly passionate for the things of Jesus and is fighting hard to show this generation all the ways He is still completely relevant to our lives. She is one of the boldest people I know and will never shy away from doing anything wild and crazy for Jesus. She is a truth bomb and if you let her she will explode your life with Biblical truths that will change your life. She is truly

amazing and one of the best people I know."
- Leah Schuster of Wagga Wagga, NSW Australia

"All good days start with putting on a blue denim button up. In our case, the matching denim shirts we wore was the beginning to a deep connection that would last throughout our childhood, teen years, and now as we navigate our adult lives. Like the old loyal denim, our friendship has become a symbol of honesty and love. Tori is that one true friend who never goes out of style. She is unwavering and courageous, which is funny because she was a shy little thing as a child. She can be a bit too trusting at times; however, she isn't afraid to confront and set things straight! I know that no matter what curve balls are pitched our way she will always be that constant steady swing ready to hit the ball into the stands. The world should also know if someone like Victoria Rich is willing to throw herself out there in a raw and somewhat embarrassing way, it's because she felt an urging within her soul. The beginning of something bigger than herself was brewing and needed to be released."
- Beth Glazer of Nashville, TN

"Victoria Rae' is like none other. A powerful Jesus loving woman who isn't afraid to change the world. This book is only a snippet of the wisdom that God has poured into her heart. Be ready for more because well, we've dated a lot of losers."
- Whitney Gruver of St Louis, MO

"Tori is a dynamic woman and even greater sister. She is bold and courageous and not afraid to shout her truth from the rooftops! That is one of the reasons I love her so... Be prepared to follow her journey of inspiration and triumph. This book has been patiently awaiting its debut, and I couldn't be more delighted for you to read the wisdom and comedic insight she will share! Follow Tori into her journey of purity. And learn why it's so precious and powerful as God's daughters to maintain it."

- Yesi Gonzalez of San Diego, CA

"Victoria brings fun, creativity, and laughter to every situation. Tori has rescued me from being smashed in a mosh pit at a screamo band concert, and is the most fun partner at the gym. Not only is Victoria one of the funniest people I know, but she is also one of the most loyal friends that you could ever have. She will always fight for you to be the best that you can be, and will encourage you to strive for more."

- Rebecca Dukes of Browder, KY

*Jesus, I thank you. Without your pursuit
of my heart I would be lost.*

*Mom and Dad, thank you for always keeping me in
check even when I wanted you to shut up. I love you.*

*Bri, thank you for helping me finish and perfect
this project to the best of our abilities.*

Josh, thank you for protecting me. You're the best little brother.

*To all my Good Girls, thank you for standing with
me as we pursue this life of purity together.*

Contents

FOREWORD

I first met Victoria Rich years ago through her CRAVE event in San Diego. It was beyond evident that she has a great passion for helping teens and young adults live radically free of drug, alcohol and sexual promiscuity by pointing them to Jesus.

Victoria is one of the most authentic people I've ever met. She is sold out for the Lord and wants everyone to know it so she can bring Him glory. Victoria never speaks from a place of judgment or condemnation; rather, she shares a message of faith in Jesus with a real and raw perspective that comes from compassion and love.

I have had the privilege of participating in a couple of CRAVE events and watching the Lord work through Victoria to change lives. In the same way CRAVE helps young people party with purpose, I truly believe this book will help them enter into relationships with purpose.

The book's subtitle says it all. This is one big sex talk. But it's not your mother's sex talk, your pastor's sex talk or even your teacher's sex talk. This is a sex talk from the perspectives of those who have lived it.

Victoria holds nothing back on the pages you are about to read. She speaks honestly, sharing her own story of failed relationships, the mistakes she has made and the lies she has believed. She weaves in stories of those she has met along the way – many of whom fell into the common traps of believing a significant other will "fix" them or bring ultimate joy and completion. She doesn't shy away from the messy realities of our sinful desires and the situations so many face in today's lustful dating culture. But in the end, Victoria reminds us of truth – Jesus is the only thing that satisfies.

Perhaps this book resonates so much with me because I have been there. Like so many, I spent years seeking love in all the wrong places and trying to fill the void left by the sudden and premature death of my earthly father, who was my world. I was a Daddy's Girl.

I so wanted to be cherished by someone the way he cherished me. As a result, I entered into a relationship too soon, married at 18 and paid the price with a divorce. My response? I jumped right into the arms of someone else, before that relationship ended.

I didn't want to be alone. It was my greatest fear. So I married again only to end up divorced again 6 years later.

I felt like the biggest failure, yet I couldn't stop in my pursuits. I married a third time but for all the wrong reasons.

The next three years were the worst time of my life. I was living in my own hell on earth. My then-husband cheated on me multiple times. He treated me like trash. He disrespected me in a way no one ever has or ever should. Slowly I began believing the lies that this is what I deserved … this was God's punishment for me.

Yet in my lowest moment, God met me. In that time where I felt more alone and more of a failure than I ever had, He was there, ready to love me and fill the void. I realized He'd been there all along wanting that and He just needed me to let go of that tangible person who I was trying to find to fill the void.

When I finally let go, it forever changed me.

After my final divorce, I spent time alone with God. To this day, that period in my life holds some of my greatest memories. I encountered the Jesus that walked on water and healed the sick. I allowed Jesus to fill my void and touch my heart and let Him pour into who I am called to be and who He sees me rather than who I believed I was because of the things I had done. I was done doing it my way.

Like Victoria and those whose stories are in this book, God got me back up after all these failures. He lifted me up and helped me move forward. He revealed that He had something better for my life (Today, I have a husband who loves me only second to Jesus. He cherishes me and protects my heart the way a husband should. I truly felt God's grace in a way I never had before him giving me Sean.)

That is what this book is all about. It isn't about sex. It isn't about finding "the one." It's about embracing the loving God who is waiting for you and ready to love you completely.

- Lynsi Snyder
Owner and President of In-N-Out Burger

armyoflove.com

Mission: **To bring together followers of Christ**

We bring together followers of Christ for training and empowerment to help them fulfill their purpose by utilizing their gifts to serve others. We deploy this "army of love" to minister directly to, and provide ministry tools and referrals for people in need.

I remember when my mom had "*The Talk*" with me.

We were driving home from my orthodontist appointment, I must have been around 11 years old. It was dark outside, and we had quite a long drive home. I still wonder why she chose that night.

She looked at me and said, "Tori, I have something I need to talk to you about..." *Gulp,* I had no clue what she was preparing herself to tell me. She seemed extremely serious. So, in silence, I waited for what came next... I can't recall every word she said. I mostly recall her saying, "A man's *'penis'* goes into a woman's *'vagina'*..."

In shock and horror I began to ask, *"How in the world could that ever happen?! How would anything fit in that tiny little hole?! Why do girls want it to go in there of all places?! What if you pee on them? I don't understand?!"*

My mom went on to explain, *"It fits in there perfectly, Tori. Not really sure how, but your body just makes a way for it. God designed your body to be joined with a man's."*

I WAS COMPLETELY, and utterly, terrified! That would certainly hurt! How in the world was that even possible?! I was disgusted, and I thought to myself, I will *NEVER* want that to happen to me. (haha)

My mom was so nervous as she told me about the birds and the bees, she missed our exit, and drove 118 miles out of the way! Needless to say, it made for a pretty long conversation… Poor mom…

Thank God my Mother had *"the talk"* with me. Here is my talk to you, dear good girls:

I've never been one to beat around the bush, so let's just get right to it. The words of this book are not meant to make you feel cozy or comfortable. Rather, these words are meant to provoke you to a different way of living. I want you to experience real change. I want you to realize your value as a Woman, and a daughter of the most high God. This won't be another boring, unrealistic dating book, with 5 steps to finding the right guy. These pages are not filled with senseless religious lingo that no one understands. (unless, like me, you were raised in church.) This book is realistic, and based on real life circumstances. It's simply real. I will tell you secrets about myself, my friends, and ALL OF THE IDIOTIC GUYS we've encountered. (the ones we escaped and the ones we are still trying to escape). These secrets will reveal that just like you, we get horny, which causes us to become weak, which leads to us losing our precious virginity; then we fall for the wrong guy - and suddenly we find ourselves pregnant! (SCREAM!) Breathe…. Breathe… Breathe… Since we are pregnant and starving, we settle for date nights at White Castle, and because he's so hot and steamy and we are more horny than ever… Yes, we love Jesus with all of our hearts, even though we've messed up more times than we can count! Yes, we are just like you, believing for the man God has designed for us, but we become impatient during the process! We are real women living in the real world trying to hold on to our purity. It's not easy being the opposite of *"easy"*, I'm just sayin'.

Let's get real though. In the world we live in, it is extremely hard for a young woman to hold on to her purity. Together, we are going to explore how we can accomplish this. I'll show you how I've held on to my virginity for 26 years, while remaining attractive and not losing my mind in the process!

I pray my words are raw and uncut like our reality TV shows, our rap songs, and my personal favorite, our Bible. It doesn't get any more real than the story of a man named (King) David who killed a friend just to sleep with his wife whom he saw bathing naked from his rooftop! God labeled him a man after His own heart, after all the messed up stuff he did. WOW! Listen, I'll go as far as I feel I have to - to get you to hear me. For if you hear me, I believe you will hear Him. And if you hear Him, I believe you will begin a journey on the road to keeping your legs closed, and your privates unexposed; and the stories of the aborted babies will soon be untold.

Introducing, Ms. Goodie 2 Shoes, the 26 year old virgin

Applause... #Sarcasm

Well... I am the Goodie 2 Shoes, the Notorious V.I.C. *(virgin in charge)*. I am the daughter of a preacher man. I am a preacher's niece, a preacher's granddaughter, a preacher's great granddaughter, and the family tree of preachers just goes on and on. Being a "PK" (Preacher's

Kid), I was expected to be perfect by most of the people around me. I had to look a certain way, talk a certain way, and live a certain way; in order to be considered *"good"* in the sight of *"church people."* My curls had to be Shirley Temple tight, and my ruffled bobby socks had to be just right. As I became older, I was expected to surround myself with certain types of people, date a certain kind of guy, or I would be labeled the *"rotten seed"* or the *"bad girl"*. Funny thing is, I am the opposite of what most people think a preacher's daughter SHOULD look like. My nose is pierced. My hair is often dyed all sorts of crazy colors. I do life with druggies, gays, rad church kids, and musicians (we all know how musicians can be sometimes, in my experience at least...) in the hopes of connecting them closer to the God who can truly rock their world. I throw Jesus parties for thousands of teenagers all over the world for a living. (Go check it out cravethemovement.com) I don't have the normal *"Christian girl"* life, and I don't plan on changing that. However, despite defying all the things I "SHOULD" be, I have found a way to be everything I was created to be in a world that is pressuring me to twerk it all out.

Here's where it starts getting real, despite being a goody goody, like everyone else on the planet, I have this one problem... I Want Sex! Or is it just love that I crave? Or are they one in the same? Why is this a problem? Well, because I am not married... It's also a problem because most "religious" people didn't talk to me about where my boundaries end. Like, is it acceptable for his fingers to penetrate, as long as it's not his, well, you know... These are things we need to explore girls, before it's too late.

The media sure isn't helping me to remain pure. Instead, they are pressuring me to try out every perverted ideology that exists! *"It's ok, girl. Just give yourself up to every guy you find attractive,"* they scream! *"Go to clubs every weekend and sleep with the first decent guy who will take you home!* "It'll be fun", they said! "It'll be liberating," they said. *"His ___ will be freedom to your thirsty soul,"* they said. *"That's how an empowered Woman in the 21st century should act!"* *"Your body; your choice!"* These are the standards in the new sex era; this is our Dark Ages. Virginity is most definitely not something we keep. Possibly, it's something we save for someone special (husband or not - that doesn't matter). The world no longer celebrates modesty, nor does it teach young girls how to cross their legs, but rather we applaud at how fast a girl can jiggle her butt on his *"D"* to a rap song. We are a bunch of screwed up little women with our legs wide open. On second thought, we are nothing like the *'Little Women' (Louisa May Alcott)* courting the wealthy neighbor's nephew who is in town for the summer. No, we are vultures, circling our prey, waiting to strike. Waiting for the first pound of flesh we can sink our teeth into! It's NOT COOL!

We will go to extreme lengths to keep our social status high. We will hide, lie, and even kill *(abortion)* just to keep the appearance of our incredibly desirable lives intact. All while continuing to have endless amounts of sex! This is how badly we want to feel accepted, loved, and full of purpose. Women, why do we choose pleasure over promise? Sexual satisfaction over sanctity? Climax over class? Promiscuity over patience? Why are you choosing his *"D"* over your children...your legacy? It seems that no matter how dirty we may feel after every episode, we keep going back for more like another relentless Netflix binge. Let's break loose from these sexual handcuffs that have us bound!

It's time to fight back! It's time for us to make purity a priority. It's time to show the world that we can be sexy and saved at the same time. Ladies, go stand on top of the kitchen counter and scream to the world, *"I AM SAVED, SANCTIFIED, FILLED WITH THE HOLY GHOST, AND SEXY! I AM WORTH WAITING FOR! I DESERVE TO BE WINED AND DINED! I WILL WAIT FOR THE ONE WHO DESERVES ALL OF ME!"*

I know there are some of you who want to be strong and independent, but simply have no idea how to make that a reality. Maybe like so many of us, you were never taught why we should keep our legs closed. This might be a brand new concept for you, and that's ok! Let me say it again, IT IS OK! We all have unique stories and are on different paths in life. Some of us grew up in a Christian home but were never given a good example to follow. Some of us had parents who didn't love us the way we needed or deserved but rather, abused us. Some of us have wonderful God fearing families but yet, we are still rebellious and wild! HA! No matter where you have come from, or how messed up you feel like you are; there is HOPE! God is not for one second worried about you, turned off by you, or ready to give up on you! He believes in you, has strength for you RIGHT NOW, and is going to show you who you are IN HIM.

By the way, writing to you, my dear friend, is helping me to stay strong! Knowing you are reading this is helping me to stay on track. Let's believe together that we can stay pure! Here we go, Good Girls!

Say this prayer with me before WE start this journey.

God please...

1. Control my need for the bad boy.

Keep your eye on the healthy soul, scrutinize the straight life; there's a future in strenuous wholeness. But the willful will soon be discarded; insolent souls are on a dead-end street. Psalm 37:37-38

2. Keep me innocent. Keep me pure... (Can you please add more pounds in the boob area?)

Who can climb Mount God? Who can scale the holy north-face? Only the clean handed, only the pure-hearted; men who won't cheat, women who won't seduce. Psalm 24:3-4 MSG

3. Real talk: You gotta help me control these horny intrusions.

No temptation has overtaken you except what is common to

mankind. And God is faithful; He will not let you be tempted beyond what you can bear. But when you are tempted, he will also provide a way out so that you can endure it. I Corinthians 10:13

4.Help me not to seem so dang "thirsty". I want to trust in you.

Commit your way to the Lord; trust in Him, and He will act. Psalm 37:5 The Lord is my strength and my shield; in Him my heart trusts, and I am helped. Psalm 28:7 When I am afraid, I put my trust in you." Psalm 56:3

5. Send me a man who will want me with my clothes on.

An excellent wife who can find? She is far more precious than jewels. Proverbs 31:10

6. Give me confidence and purpose without having to have approval from a man.

Charm is deceitful, and beauty is vain, but a woman who fears the Lord is to be praised. Proverbs 31:30

7. Enable me to fall deeply in love with you Jesus.

How precious is your unfailing love, O God! Psalm 36:7

8. Lastly, help me to stay strong, so that I can show others

the way.

As each one of you has received a gift, minister it to one another, as good stewards of the manifold grace of God. 1 Peter 4:10

...And the list goes on.

"Dear Lord, when I get to Heaven please let me bring my man, when he comes tell me that you'll let him in, father tell me if you can."

I'm sorry, but it does not work that way. I wish it did. All in all, friend, your sexy boyfriend is the last thing you'll be thinking about when standing in front of Jesus Christ.

TALK 1

Love Me Tinder

Before I tell you this story I want to make it very clear to you, dear reader, that I'm in no way knocking dating apps, or finding love on the Internet. My beloved cousin met his outstanding wife on the Internet. Also, my close friend and coworker *(who is responsible for this story I'm about to tell you)* met his wife on Tinder. Do I believe they are the exception? Yes, I absolutely do. I believe it's very rare, but very possible to find lasting love through dating apps!

The world we live in is very, very different from the times when *"courting"* someone was a normal thing to do before asking for their hand in marriage. My Grandmother would faint after hearing some of the stories my friends have told me. I knew a girl (from church) who let a massage therapist touch her inappropriately, while giving her a massage; she even let him go down on her! I'm just keeping it REAL! My Grandfather can't even watch a *Victoria's Secret* commercial without feeling like he needs to ask for forgiveness. Don't make me get out the porn statistics! (28,258 users are watching porn every second.) Our generation is very different, to say the very least, from a time when getting married at 17 was the norm. It seems we have to do a lot more searching these days before deciding on a spouse. Maybe it's because we are harder to please? Maybe we are ruined because of the "dating culture" and having the ability to trade in our men the first time a big fight happens. Maybe we have way too many options?? Instagram... Facebook... Snapchat... Tinder... Plenty of Fish... Sorry for the small rabbit trail, back to dating apps. I personally, would much rather meet my man in person, before going out with him alone...however, that didn't stop me from creating a dating profile - now did it?! Desperate times people - these were desperate times that provoked me to do very silly things.

First dates have never been my strong suit. A first date with a stranger would have to be my worst nightmare, which is why I should have never downloaded Tinder. They make me extremely nervous and my hands tend to sweat profusely, making it mega awkward if they want to hold hands. I don't really know why I get so nervous. Maybe it's because my personality is not so normal outside of a setting where I know mostly everyone or I am in control. I'm afraid people won't understand me or have a good first impression of me. When I get nervous, I get quiet, which sucks because these dudes drill you like you're prepping for their hometown date on *The Bachelor*. . . *(I despise first dates!)* Also, many times I have trusted the wrong people, and that has unfortunately landed me in a few interesting and sometimes dangerous situations. I have an uncanny ability to see the best in people. I have lived a very sheltered life. I haven't come across many psychos. Church people are my life. Good people are my life. So it's just not my first instinct to think someone is going to be off-the-wall crazy.

Soooo, here it is...

I met a guy on a dating app, who was very good looking, and who seemed to have the same beliefs that I did. So I thought maybe I should actually go on a date with him. I haven't been on one of those in a decade! *(My mother is going to be so upset when she reads this.)* Mom will probably think to herself, "Victoria Rae, you are way too pretty, too talented, too smart, and too GIFTED BY THE ALMIGHTY GOD to ever stoop so low as to try a sketchy dating app!" Anyway friends, people who seem to have everything together, actually don't have anything together all the time. I get lonely. Plus my coworker met his fiancé on this app, so I thought to myself, *WHAT THE HECK?!* My time clock is ticking! Something's gotta give!

We chatted via cellular phone call, and it was a great conversation. He seemed very spiritual, and that made me feel good about him.

I agreed to a date...

At first, he seemed alright...*(referring to his mental state of mind...)* Physically, he was built like the Rock of Gibraltar. His perfectly tanned skin glistened in the summer sun, and reminded me of the Native American warriors from Pocahontas. His big bright green eyes seemed to stare directly into the deepest parts of my soul. I could imagine he used those enchanting eyes to get what he wanted. Girl, he was very attractive! I was thanking the Lord Jesus he had created a human being to invent this glorious app called Tinder! *(Not that looks have much to do with ANYTHING, by the way!)* Anyway, his personality was very eccentric and mysterious, so of course, I liked that as well. As I always say, *"Weird is good."* I enjoyed the conversation over dinner and I was thinking to myself, *"Maybe I could actually like this guy!"* When dinner concluded, he asked if I wanted to extend the date and go see a movie. Things seemed to be going great, so I agreed.

We headed to the theater, and when we got out of the car, he abruptly mentioned that he was feeling anxious. He told me he forgot something in the car, and that he would meet me inside. At first I didn't think anything of it, then once we got inside the theater, he began to fall into people and run into walls! He grabbed my hand to hold it. Usually I would've jerked away at this stage of the game, but since he was falling all over the place *(and into innocent bystanders)*, I figured I should help the guy out.

I became frightened, as he began acting even more abnormal. He started tapping strangers on the shoulder and dying laughing about it. Women's husbands/boyfriends were looking at him like, *"Boy, you better back up!"* I began to panic. My heart was racing. A thousand thoughts were flying through my mind as I watched this guy become insanely messed up on whatever it was he took in his car. *"How the heck do I get outta here?!"*, I thought to myself as I began to search the building for exit doors. I didn't know what to do. I was afraid to leave him alone! *"What if he passed out dead in the theater?! What if he gets into a fight, and they beat his face to a pulp!"* No, I didn't owe this person anything! However, it didn't feel right leaving him alone in this obvious state of mental insanity. Not to mention, I couldn't seem to find an immediate escape. I told myself once we got into the theater to sit down, I would pretend to have to use the bathroom and simply jet out of there!

As we purchased popcorn and drinks, he continued to act absolutely crazy at the counter. Giving them $100 too much, then cursing them out for giving him the correct amount of change back. He was saying sexually offensive things to girls, dropping his popcorn and drink all over the ground, high fiving everyone that walked by, then got angry when he missed their hands. I discreetly kept my distance - watching it all take place in total shock and horror.

Finally, we struggle to get seated in the theater, and just as soon as my back hits the seat, who immediately comes walking in? The cops. My heart feels as if it's beating against the walls of my stomach! I know they are coming for him. They politely ask him to come to the hallway so they can ask him some questions. He becomes extremely violent and refuses to go with them. I'm quietly trying to disappear in my seat - literally - sinking extremely low trying to hide my head behind him in hopes they didn't realize he had a date. The cops finally, with force, convince him to get his butt up and follow them. All of a sudden I hear yelling from the hall where they took him. Screaming! Punching! Kicking! Body slamming! I'm freaking out. I've never experienced anything like this in my life! The girl in front of me turned around in disgust and whispered, *"Girl, is that your bae?!"* I'm all like, *"HECK NO!"* Feeling like a complete idiot!

Long story short, they arrested him, and I had to call

my little brother to come pick me up, who, by the way, was insanely *FURIOUS* with me. I deleted that stupid freaking app right then and never downloaded it again! How stupid I felt! *HOW HORRIBLE THAT COULD HAVE TURNED OUT FOR ME!* Even now I cringe, reminiscing about it. When we get lonely, sometimes we become desperate. No matter how together we might be or think we are, it happens to the best of us. Trust God, and only God. Loneliness is never a good enough reason to put your life at risk.

For I know the plans I have for you, declares the Lord, plans to prosper you and not harm you, plans to give you hope and a future. Jeremiah 29:11

Disclaimer: I'm not knocking dating apps, they've been very successful for so many. I have a friend, a fellow preacher's kid, who's dad pays for her eHarmony account. HAHA!

TALK 2

Sexy and Saved?

For some reason, I feel like I need to take you ALL THE BACK to the VERY BEGINNING. Before my life became this exponentially weird! Before I became tainted by this world's sexualistic ideology. Buckle up, Kids... this ride may get a little bumpy! Here We Go!

As a young girl, I was very skinny, naive and innocent in my knowledge of all things sexual. I remember one particular incident that stung me a little bit. I was with a group of kids my age, and they were making fun of my body, and the notion that I was a *"goody goody"* in their opinion. I was a feisty little thing, and I probably had a pretty brutal comeback.... (That hopefully doesn't still scar them to this day) nevertheless, they began to really tease me and make fun of the fact that I probably had never masturbated before. One girl began to tell me exactly how to do it, which made me feel very uncomfortable. It's times like those that make us want to explore our sexuality in ways we shouldn't. I remember wanting to fit in. I wanted to know what their sexual jokes meant. I considered myself to be tough, so I acted like their remarks didn't bother me, but they really did.

It was the same, as I grew older. I was constantly ridiculed for being - what they felt was the *"goody two shoes"* or the *"saint."* I saw other teenage girls (*whose vaginas were perfectly shaved, because they were already having sex)*, and I always felt out of place. I could never relate to them. I'm so thankful for that now. Most of those girls have already gone through a divorce and have had to deal with their husbands cheating on them. It's crazy now, to look at those women, who once made fun of me for my lifestyle. It saddens me.

My father was raised in a very strict Southern Pentecostal Church, where women weren't allowed to shave their legs, cut their hair, or wear pants. I was talking to my sweet Memaw (who was a minister's wife and only allowed to wear white) about her memories growing up in the church. She began to tell me in her slow, smooth southern voice that my dad wasn't allowed to be involved in sports, and that they certainly could never have a TV in their home. Because if they did, they would surely be condemned to hellfire and brimstone.

This is not the case for all Christians of course. I grew up Pentecostal, and we were far less strict. However, in the majority of churches, many women are handed down more rules and regulations than men and are given less grace. They are told they have to dress and look a certain way in order to be *"holy"* in the sight of God. Your relationship with God should not be contingent on a set of rules, but rather about a relationship built on unconditional love and mutual respect. I am completely in agreement with modesty, and hey, if your relationship with Jesus causes you to never cut your hair or vow to dress a certain way, more power to you.... just never allow it to become only about the rules. God wants your heart - not your leg hair.

The Lord does not look at the things people look at. People look at the outward appearance, but the Lord looks at the heart. 1 Samuel 16:7 NIV

(Do you sometimes feel like the world portrays *"goody goody/church girls"* as being *unattractive, homely, repulsive, unpleasant* or maybe a bit *nerdy*?) I mean we've all heard music lyrics that make the good girl look like she's no fun, right? Example: When I think of how the world views *"us"*, I see a tall skinny girl, wearing oversized glasses and a sweater vest. A skirt dragging the floor, and white (but muddy) old lady tennis shoes. She says, *"You're going to Hell!"*, to every fly girl who passes by her. If you see that same girl, let's erase that picture in our minds. Replace that picture with this one. You do not have to wear a sports bra, under your sweater vest, and granny panties, under your skirt (that extends to the ground), in order to maintain your virginity; or to be categorized as a *"good girl"*. As a matter of fact, God doesn't want or expect you to appear that way! Nor do you have to fit into a certain mold that SOME Christians, and most of the media have created for you. THE ONLY MOLD you were meant to fit in, is the one made for you by the One who created you.

Is the girl with the sweater vest and long skirt unattractive to God? NO, you crazy person! We are all incredibly beautiful to our God. He wants you to be YOU, and no one else! If He wanted another Susie, He wouldn't have made you. There isn't another you on the planet.

There wasn't a you 200 years ago, and there will never be another you again. You are the only one like you...there is and never will be anyone just like you. You were placed on this planet at this specific time for a very specific purpose, and if you cannot simply be you, then it's been a complete waste of not only your time but God's time as well. If you dig crazy big hair and neon lipstick, then go for it girl! Don't allow yourself to feel as if religion is a box for you to fit into. Jesus came and broke every box and barrier so that we, His daughters, could live creatively in His freedom as He created us!

For it is for freedom that Christ has set us free. Galatians 5:1

Allow me to take a few moments of your time to rant about who you are and why you are undeniably the apple of God's eye. READY?

1. You are an original, a stand out. It's just that simple, really. You weren't meant to fit into anyone else's ideal of what they think you should be. There has never been another you to ever exist since the beginning of time!

2. You are a one of a kind woman created by the almighty God. You aren't expected to be anyone else but YOU!

4. You have a story that was meant to change lives! You have a voice! Let go of insecurity and scream your story to the world!

5. (and if that's not enough) You have gifts and talents that were placed deep down inside of you, to shake the world around you! Start exploring and using those gifts!

Believe and know how special you truly are. Write these points down and place them where you can see them everyday. REMIND yourself of the amazing woman you are! It will help... I PROMISE. Until you believe those things about yourself, how do you ever imagine someone else believing them? It's time to transform yourself from the inside out - baby girl. When you start believing you are unique and one of a kind, you will begin to attract men that believe the same thing about you. When we are insecure and unaware of our existence, we put ourselves in a scary position to become hurt and abused; because we simply don't know our true worth.

The question isn't, *"How good or Holy can I be?"*, or *"How long can I remain a virgin?"* It's more, *"How can I be the very best person I can be - the person HE designed me to be?"*

Now hear me out, I'm not saying that there is anything wrong with wearing a sweater vest *(my mom loves sweater vests)* or a skirt to the floor, like the women in my father's old church. If that's you, rock it, baby, rock it! What I am simply trying to say is, "You can look hot and still be a *"good girl!"* You can be sexy and still be respectful and classy. Quit letting other people leave a bad taste in your mouth about what is *"good."*

Jesus, in my opinion, digs my crazy clothes. Why? He's the one that created me to love crazy fashion. It's a part of who I am. I can be hot and a good girl at the same time.... and so can you. Sexy and Saved at the same time,

Good Girl! I believe that God is proud when I look hot! He loves when I feel confident and empowered as the amazing woman that I am! There's no way God wants to hide you under baggy clothes, insecurity, and fear! He wants to show his amazing baby off to the world.

Such confidence we have through Christ before God. 2 Corinthians 3:4

Being boring and unattractive does not make you *"holy"* or *"godly"*; it simply limits the gifts you possess and the beauty God has placed inside of you. Being a Good Girl has everything to do with the heart, and nothing to do with anyone else's religious ideas of what I should wear, or how many times I can say 'bless her heart'. *(after gossiping about a friend.)* Let's get real…

I praise you because I am fearfully and wonderfully made; your works are wonderful, I know that full well. Psalms 139:14

TALK 3

Good Girls Don't Have Fun

Even as a young adult, I still find myself rebelling against what people want and think I should be. I'm thankful that God doesn't see my uniqueness as rebellion, yet rather, He sees it as obedience to what He has called me to be. I want to tell you a story from when I was a young girl. Even then it seemed as if I always stood out just a bit. I'm so thankful now as I look back at certain circumstances, that my spirit was never broken. I'm thankful that God protected my desire to be different. I was 14 years old and going to a private school at the time. We were at some kind of weird camp where hundreds of home schools and private schools would come together to compete in sports, art, music etc. When I say it was weird, I truly mean it was weird. Girls were required to wear dreadful seamless skirts that had to cover their ankles and long sleeve shirts. I was a runner at the time and had to wear culottes. *(laugh if you remember culottes)* Yeah, they are pretty much like wearing two large skirts around each leg. Go purchase some at your local Kmart and try running a marathon in those suckers! I entered the singing contest, and to be honest, I felt pretty confident about it. There was no way these weirdos knew how to blow. *(No pun intended.)* I remember belting out the lyrics to Amazing Grace in front of the judges, and seriously knocking it out of this Amish-looking park. The judges glared at me the entire time with this evil judgmental look in their eyes. Unaware of what they were actually thinking, I thought to myself, *"Maybe their faces look like that all the time. Like they want to stab everybody with a crucifix. They must be miserable, dried up old ladies, that are a part of an awful soprano section at a Catholic church. I would probably look that way too."*

So I sang on. I remember getting to the end of my performance and feeling so accomplished when suddenly one of the judges yells at me, *"YOU'RE DISQUALIFIED, YOUNG LADY!"* I said, for what biiiii... Just kidding... I said in a very sweet voice, *"For what, Ma'am."* I WANTED THAT TROPHY! She then went on to tell me that my long skirt was denim, therefore I was immediately disqualified. To be honest, I'm still ticked off about that to this day. Sometimes, religious people can be freakin' pathetic. I remember in that moment thinking, *"I will never be like these horrible people, who don't even act like the Jesus they proclaim to love."* You know what? It wasn't even about the long denim skirt. It was the heart and attitude behind their actions. Why didn't they tell me when I walked in that my skirt wasn't the right material? It was embarrassing for goodness sake! **BE YOU!** When you know who you are in Christ, don't let anyone stand in your way. Wear your denim skirt and belt your heart out no matter what looks people may have on their faces!

By the way, I won first place in the photography contest. I remember my dad leaning down and whispering to me in the middle of the ceremony, *"You don't even know how to take pictures, that's God's favor, Tori. He's letting you know you are number 1 in his eyes." "Oh, Dad…"* I said as I smiled and took that trophy home to place on the shelf.

Maybe our view of *"good girls"* has nothing to do with attire. Maybe we just picture them boring and incapable of having any fun. People have always asked me questions like this, *"So like, what do you do besides go to church?"* As if being a young Christian girl means: we live at church and memorize hymnals all day and all night. If we do manage to have fun, then it looks something like scrapbooking all of our favorite scriptures, or learning how to sew bonnets for our future children; who rest in our virgin wombs. In actuality, if any of those that are asking silly questions, stepped inside my life or the lives of my friends for 24 hours, they would be blasted away with the fun machine! *(that was so corny…haha)* **You are allowed to have fun!**

We can have fun and still remain "good" and "pure". When we become a Christian, it doesn't mean that our emotions and personalities have to disappear. They are actually made COMPLETE, because Jesus is the center of them now. Anything is possible through you now, because Jesus is within you. Your hands are His hands. Your feet are His feet. Trust in him to be with you always. Step into Holy confidence and be the Woman God has created you to be! There is nothing more freeing and liberating than being in His presence and in the center of His purpose. He is the founder of Joy. He is the creator of Happiness. Anything that doesn't come straight from Him is *counterfeit*. **Regain** freedom from the fake! Now live in complete freedom to be who you were truly created to be!

For you created my inmost being; you knit me together in my mother's womb. I praise you because I am fearfully and wonderfully made; your works are wonderful, I know that full well. Psalm 139:13-14

My God...

Our God is creative. *In the beginning God created the heavens and the earth. Genesis 1:1* I mean honestly, look around! Everything you see, He has created and is yet creating! My mind reverts to *Cirque Du Soleil* or *Michael Jackson's* eccentric talent. Our Jesus created it all! Satan is not able to create. He only takes what God has already created and perverts it. So why would we put Jesus in this small boring brown box, only believing He does things in a monotonous fashion. My Jesus does not only dish out plain vanilla, He has every flavor in the book. I promise you Jesus won't be found in your small religious brown box, because our magnificent God can not be restricted to a mere box, especially a boring one. Jesus is **colorful**! You better *swag* that box out! Look at the people He created, different sizes, colors, and personalities. They are all incredibly beautiful to Him.

So God created mankind in his own image, in the image of God he created them; male and female he created them. Gen 1:27

He made you to be like Him. You are filled with all

kinds of crazy gifts and talents that God has given you for His purpose. Explore the gifts He's placed inside of you. You are the only one of your kind; created perfectly to fulfill the task He has called you to fulfill. If you find yourself in a place where you have no clue what your talents are or what God has even placed you on this earth for, begin to fall in love with the one who created them, and He in His own magnificent mysterious way will begin to reveal Himself to you. Suddenly, you will begin to find your true purpose and meaning in life, because when you find who He is - you will find who you are. He is the reason we exist. He is the Alpha and the Omega, our beginning and our end. He formed us in our Mother's womb, and He will surely be the one we return to when we leave this Earth. Only if *"y'all stop acting like hoes!"* (just kidding)

Find Him so you can, in return find yourself! He has plans for you far greater than you could ever ask for or imagine!

Now Him who is able to do immensely more than all we ask, think, or imagine, according to His power that is at work within us. Ephesians 3:20

God wants you to discover who you are in HIM before you decide to give your life over to a man. He's too jealous of a God *(For the Lord your God is a consuming fire, a jealous God. Deut 4:24)* to share you with someone that will use you, abuse you, or not recognize your true value! If you are His daughter He will protect you from bad relationships. Listen, it is going to be difficult enough already for you to discover who you are in Jesus dealing with your own personal flesh. If you are merging yourself with someone else *(banging it out)* you will have a far more difficult time! There's more to sex than mere skin on skin. Sex is as much a spiritual mystery as physical fact. As written in Scripture, *"The two become one."* *1 Corinthians 6:19 MSG* When you have sex with someone, you are literally becoming one with them. I can't imagine how difficult it would be if you were giving yourself sexually to more than one person. How confusing that would be for your spirit! Jesus is the only man you can give yourself to and find out who you truly are. He wants us fully emerged in the pursuit of getting to know Him before we add another human to the equation ESPECIALLY sexually. It's hard enough staying fully focused on a holy, purified life. Sex will mess you UP in the wrong timing, outside of marriage.

There's more to sex than mere skin on skin. Sex is as much spiritual mystery as physical fact. As written in Scripture, "The two become one." Since we want to become spiritually one with the Master, we must not pursue the kind of sex that avoids commitment and intimacy, leaving us more lonely than ever — the kind of sex that can never "become one." There is a sense in which sexual sins are different from all others. In sexual sin we violate the sacredness of our own bodies, these bodies that were made for God-given and God-modeled love, for "becoming one" with another. Or didn't you realize that your body is a sacred place, the place of the Holy Spirit? Don't you see that you can't live however you please, squandering what God paid

such a high price for? The physical part of you is not some piece of property belonging to the spiritual part of you. God owns the whole works. So let people see God in and through your body.
1 Corinthians 6:16-20

It is no longer I who live, but Christ lives in me. Galatians 2:20

I'm not saying we have to be absolutely perfect with everything figured out and money in the bank to find ourselves and our soul mates. However, what I am saying is this: we must have Jesus if we want any of it to work the way it is supposed to, and more importantly, if we want to end up with the right person.

People are divorcing like they are still in middle school, trying to decide which crush to be with for the week! Millions of children go to sleep with broken hearts, because mommy and daddy didn't take the time to work on themselves; or put God first before adding someone else into the mix! Let's stop being selfish: only caring about our personal needs, and realize there is a God in heaven whose heart is breaking, and a man out there somewhere who is counting on us to get ourselves straight. Our future children are relying on us to get them here safely to this earth ....what an amazing thought it truly is, that somewhere in Heaven, our daughters and sons await the day when we can bring them to earth with God's permission. They hope that mommy isn't addicted to drugs or daddy isn't infected with an awful disease, so that they can truly enter this world pure and innocent. (Your baby's cry, *"Mama, please don't make me pass through*

that infested vagina of yours! Hello Doc, C-section please!")
We have to wake up and get ourselves together!

Unlike so many women in our society, Mary knew the worth of her purity and did not negotiate or put it up for grabs. She was chosen by God to carry within her the hope of the world, Jesus Christ. Why did God choose a virgin? Why did God choose Mary? We will never know all the reasons, but one is obvious and sure: Jesus had to be born of a pure vessel. I love that Mary was waiting before she ever had any idea an angel would appear to her and tell her she would conceive a son, the Son of God. God wants to do mind blowing things in your life… but first and foremost, He cares about the purity of your heart. I have to tell myself often, *"Tori, remember all that God has promised you! Don't get your hands dirty with this or that, it will only prolong the journey to your dreams!"*

He that has clean hands and a pure heart… Psalm 24:4

Think about this, because of Mary's willingness to wait and furthermore, carry and give birth to Jesus, we can be forgiven for our floozy ways and be used by God like she was. Without her wait, where would we be? Her purity was far more important then she knew. Your purity is far more important than you know. You carry within you the *future* of the world around you. You carry within your womb the **legacy** of your family, the **hope** of your family. Why would we ever let impostures touch us, ruin our legacy, and spill his seed on our hope? I don't mean to get all *"deep"* on you right now but, seriously, every time you let the D enter your womb you are giving someone permission to touch your legacy *(the eggs within your womb)*. Literally...physically...not to mention spiritually. You are taking a chance with your future. You are putting your legacy up for grabs. *"Woman, you hold the future of your family in your womb. Quit letting dogs inside to piss all over it."*

I get emotional thinking about Mary, the 15 year old, who was chosen to carry the hope of the world in her womb. I can't begin to imagine the embarrassment she had to endure, while trying to explain that she was indeed still a virgin, and that she was chosen to carry the Son of God - in her womb. Let me give you a little understanding. I know that in the times we live in, it is considered normal for a woman to become pregnant outside of marriage, but in Mary's time; women were dragged into the streets by the hair of their head, and stoned by the people of the city for such an abominable act.

She stayed strong. She never swayed. I have no doubt there were hardships, tears, and anger but nonetheless, she kept the goal in mind and gave birth to the Son of God. Marvelous! What else is there to say...

And Mary said: "My soul glorifies the Lord and my spirit rejoices in God my Savior, for He has been mindful of the humble state of His servant. From now on all generations will call me blessed, for the Mighty One has done great things for me. Holy is His name.

Luke 1:46-49

23

The First Touch

At 17 years old I knew without a shadow of a doubt my purity would never be tampered with. I was in control. Never once had little miss *"goody goody"* ever been tempted with sex, no, not I! That was until this preacher's son...

(Man, these boys still try to get into my panties, even while their daddies are behind the pulpit! CRY FACE! Where are the real men of God at!?)

He's a worship leader and preacher yet he still begs for me to take my clothes off after church. What a horny joke!

Prior to this mega horny preacher's son, my good girl ways were well intact. I was the legit, real, untouched *"Good Girl"* *(virgin princess)* until this fake booty Christian boy introduced me to a feeling I had never had before.

I can still remember the first time he touched me in an inappropriate place... I'm not going to lie to you and pretend like it didn't feel great; it did. It is supposed to feel that way, BUT when done out of the context of marriage it can cause us MUCH premature pain that God does not want us to have to deal with at such a young age. PLUS, once you get that fire burning you can't hardly put it out!

This first time feeling occurred in the back seat of a dark car, *(of course)* where my parents, *(poor innocent souls)* were in the front seat. I was curled up asleep in the back, when he awakened me with his hand in a place that felt very pleasurable. I pushed his hand away, but it soon returned. By the fifth time his hand returned, I didn't have the strength to push him away. How could one gather the strength to stop something that felt so FREAKIN GOOD! *GIRLS, DO NOT LET BOYS CROSS BOUNDARIES! YOU WILL NOT HAVE THE STRENGTH TO SAY NO FOREVER!*

I was young and very **green** to anything sexual. At this time in my life, it was a HUGE deal if a guy touched my butt, so you can imagine what a major deal this was to me. That's the way it should be and still is as far as I'm concerned. We had been dating for a few months and I felt like I was falling in love for the first time. I guess I probably was.... maybe. It felt like I had possibly found the one. *GAG.* I mean come on, his parents were pastors and they were best friends with my family. *Blah blah blah.* This was great, right?! Who was I fooling ... a bunch of church people, that's who. I soon began to understand that it would be nearly impossible to stay away from the feeling he had given me. It was like a curse, a trap.

Guilt began to overtake me the more I let him touch me, and introduce me to new things. I remember one time in particular; I had to preach for my father on a Sunday. He was on vacation and left me in charge. I called my best friend to the office before the service started and spilled my guts. I broke completely down. I began crying big tears of guilt and disappointment in myself. I laid out all the dirty details on what was going on and how I felt I couldn't go out there and preach. Being the incredible friend that she was/is, she calmed me down and prayed for me. I felt the forgiveness, acceptance, and peace of God and knew I couldn't let that lifestyle continue. I got through the condemnation and let God heal me and I walked out onto that stage, by the grace of God. No, I wasn't having sex per say, but what's the difference, right? Filth is filth. Sin is sin. I was caught all up in it and it wasn't right. But who could I tell?! I was suffocating. I was supposed to be a perfect pastor's daughter who was dating the perfect pastor's son! I carried the weight of my own judgment and the fear of everyone else's. I didn't have many people I could trust this truth with, without them freaking out and losing all respect for me. So, I just kept it to myself mostly.

Time went on and I gave in to his hands many, many times. Let me tell you about this dude. He was bad. Good Lord... The most jealous person I've ever met to this day in fact. I put up with so much freakin' crap as a poor innocent teenager, it was sickening. Do you ever look back at your past relationships and wonder how you could have been so stupid?! It happens to all us, I promise it does. He wouldn't let me hang with my friends without completely blowing my phone up. I couldn't speak to the opposite sex, without him calling me out as a flirt or whore. I hated him, but I loved him at the same time. I shudder to think about how Jesus felt watching me put up with all of his ignorance. He is so good to clean us up

27

every time we allow ourselves to be consumed with the most horrible of things or people.

This dude looked good on the outside. He had all the right things going on in his life, but no one knew that he tormented me with jealousy and envy. I didn't know, while he was controlling me with jealousy and accusing me of being a whore, *(a whore? I'm a freakin virgin you jerk!)* he was having sex with minors the entire time. I realize now that he was only calling me the very thing he was. I look back and see what a pure heart I had even though I had made mistakes, the biggest one being with that idiot. The guilt I felt because of it and the way I tried to do what was right over and over again, showed my true heart. I was so young. So new to boys in general and so in love with Jesus and he took care of me the entire time.

I remember one evening he was driving my friend and I through a drive-thru Taco Bell, and my best friend who was in the back seat couldn't decide what to order. *(She did this often)* All of a sudden he screamed at her and told her to, *"Freaking hurry up! God, you're so stupid!"* In a screaming rage, he ordered without knowing what she wanted. I was boiling hot tamale mad. I tried my best to keep myself from slamming his head into the steering wheel, but man did I want to so badly! I resisted from doing that, thanks to the almighty God, Jesus. We arrive at the window and she hands him about 20 quarters to pay her bill... *Ha.* He made a smart-alecky remark and I lost it. I acted like I was taking the quarters from him and then proceeded to throw them as hard as I could at his face. *"No one talks to my friends like that!"* I screamed. I am still so very proud of myself for doing that. :) *(High five!)*

That's just one incident where he was a complete ass. That word is in the Bible when referring to a donkey. So I'm using it... thanks. I could write you a hundred pages about how he emotionally abused me with jealousy and anger but he's not worth your time or mine.

When we finally broke up *(because he cheated on me)* after dating for 2 years, I remember thinking I could never fall in love with anyone else. Girl, I was over his ugly behind in about a month flat. It's never as hard as you think it's going to be! We don't live in a movie. We live in the real world, and with God's help we can conquer any emotion or feeling we may have. I'm not saying it was easy, because it most certainly was not and I missed him. I became lonely, but it was easier than I ever imagined it would be and I'm so incredibly thankful God snatched me out of his filthy hands. Satan is the king of lies. He will keep you trapped for years bound in fear. Fear that you will be too lonely or won't be able to find anyone else. Don't live in fear! Break free from the abuse. The jealousy. The envy. You Are a Queen!

The thief comes only to steal, kill, and destroy. I have come that they may have life and have it to the full. John 10:10

The god of peace will SOON crush Satan under YOUR feet. Romans 16:20

I've fought with temptation for a long time. I've won many battles and lost many battles. Your heart is the hardest thing to control, because it feels right a lot of the time, and who doesn't want to follow their heart? You must make sure you are following God's heart and not your own. Believe it or not, your heart is sinful, filthy, selfish, and insecure. Only with God is our heart pure. Your emotions and your heart will lead you astray. Stand firm on the word of God. It's alright if your heart fails you, you don't need it... You only need the heart of God. His heart will never fail you.

A fool gives full vent to his spirit... Prov 29:11

I've stood back and watched as God has taken my mistakes and turned them into beautiful testimonies that I hope are moving you right now. Your stories will do the same for so many. There is so much power in YOU telling your story. Start telling it, Good Girl.

And they have conquered him by the blood of the Lamb and by the word of their testimony, for they loved not their lives even unto death. Revelation 12:11

Just Jesus.

I dreamed of Jesus once... I want to tell you about the incredibly real experience but I suppose I should save it for another time. (Go watch "Have Fun Fishing" the film on my social media accounts) I've always been very close to Him. I honestly can't remember a time when I didn't feel Him next to me. Well, except for when I have done things I'm not supposed to, like hardcore make out sessions in cars late at night.

Jesus is how I have made it this far. At a very young age, He was the reason I decided to wait.

I want you to know who Jesus truly is, because He is the only way you can successfully live pure. I want you to experience Jesus beyond just what we've seen from the pretty picture hanging on the wall. I want you to know His personality. His character. His joy. His anger. His strength. Most people do not want to take the time to truly know Him. It's sad but so true. Why you ask, because they are comfortable in their religious mindsets. They don't have to grow inside their boring box. They have laid down a few quilts and a pillow and are carelessly sleeping through their Christian lives. *A set of rules is easier than a relationship.* Here's the thing, with a set of rules you don't get to enjoy any of the benefits you obtain with being in a relationship with someone. It's like having a father that pays child support, but isn't in the picture. We shouldn't want to just pay our dues and miss out on knowing the most incredible man to ever own Heaven and Earth. *We NEED to WANT to know Him.*

It's easy to think of Jesus as some angelic figure far away who would never listen to rap music or make a joke. It's also unsatisfying (at least to me). If we perceive Jesus as this person that is *NOTHING* like us, then we will never feel comfortable in our own skin. We will never find out who we truly are if we don't know who our father is, and the purpose He has for us. We will feel enslaved to religion. Entangled to everyone else's opinion of who He is, and we won't even know Him for ourselves. Jesus doesn't want religion with you; He wants a relationship with you. Believe it or not He's more interested in you than anything else in the world. The Bible tells us that Jesus would leave everything just to come find you.

What do you think? If any man has a hundred sheep, and one of them has gone astray, does he not leave the ninety-nine on the mountains and go and search for the one that is straying? If it turns out that he finds it, truly I say to you, he rejoices over it more than over the ninety-nine which have not gone astray... Matthew 18:12,13

He's been pursuing you since you were born. Romancing you. Ladies, when we can know our Jesus on an intimate level, we will truly be able to find exactly who we are and show it off to the world. For when we begin to know our Father, we begin to truly know ourselves. It is in that state where we find true contentment.

Get rid of the religious version of Jesus and find out who He truly is on your own.

We love because He first loved us. 1 John 4:19

A relationship brings meaning to the reason of having religion. People can get religion from a lot of different false gods all over the world, but Jesus is the only God who will give back to the people who give themselves to Him.

You can offer up breakfast, lunch, and dinner to Buddha, but he's never going to get up and eat it. No matter how many times you pray to Allah, he'll never answer you back. Jesus responds to our every need. Religion can offer you a lot of rules and guidelines, but those rules by themselves cannot offer you any intimacy. Rules and guidelines are needed most definitely, but without love and a relationship with Jesus; they mean nothing. Jesus offers freedom for us. He doesn't cause us to be perfect - just forgiven. My relationship with Jesus and the love I have for Him has been the driving force for me to wait. I love him enough to keep the promises I've made. When you've made a covenant with someone you are completely in love with, it's far easier than trying to keep a covenant with someone you are not in love with and do not have a relationship with. Our relationship with Jesus should be viewed as a marriage, because that's truly what it is. When we say yes we become married to Him. Don't let religion be your relationship with Jesus. Experience Him for yourself. He will be the loudest voice in your head when you're pressured most to go back on the promises you've made. Be strong and courageous in the power of His might.

I was reading a book once, *The Beautiful Outlaw*, when I really began to see the personality of my Jesus unfold. It really opened my eyes to His humor and how we can find the personality of Jesus in our everyday lives. I remember the author talking about how his animals would pop up during the most intense family fights and just do something hilarious. I believe Jesus' personality and even His humor is all around us. We just have to look around and be open to exploring Him. We have to be open to knowing Him on a level we've never experienced before. We need to realize that He cares about every little detail of our lives, small or huge! The moment your heart is crushed and you don't see how you will ever love again, is the time that He is waiting for you to realize He is right beside you wiping away every tear.

When we can discover who we truly are as a daughter of the king and figure out what makes us unique, what gives us fiery passion, what makes our blood boil. When we can let go of all the negative preconceived ideas of what others have said about us, then we can find ourselves and when we find ourselves in Jesus, we will find the man on Earth He has for us. Jesus has put so many talents, gifts, and abilities inside of you that only you have! Don't limit yourself to someone else's standards. Talk with Jesus. Hear for yourself what He has to say about you! He made you the way He wanted you to be... *perfectly imperfect.*

Like a Child...

I can look at the status of my relationship with Jesus by looking at the type of man I'm falling for at the time. I remember as a very young girl, all I wanted in life was to evangelize the world with my two best friends, Rebecca and Beth. To love Jesus with all my heart was all I ever cared about... I remember telling my dad one day in the kitchen, *"Oh Dad, I just love God's presence so much, I wish I could be there every second of every day."*

What does the Bible say about children? It says that we must first become as a child if we want to enter into the kingdom of Heaven. I remember my girls and I saying, *"We will never get married! We will give our lives to Jesus for as long as we live!"* Of course those feelings have changed, but the passion I had for my Jesus was so innocently beautiful.

I tell you the truth, unless you turn from your sins and become like little children, you will never enter the kingdom of Heaven. Matthew 18:3

I believe that if we desire true contentment in our relationships and in our personal lives, we must fall in love with Jesus in a way that our only desire is to please Him. If we live this way, in return everything else will fall into place, and instead of being unbalanced *(consuming ourselves in relationships that were never meant for us)*; our eyes will be open and our hearts won't fall for anything counterfeit so easily. When we can get to this place, I believe we set ourselves up for success in our relationships, and I also believe that God will send us our companion.

I'm not by any means saying we have to reach a point of perfection before God sends us the man He has for us... that will never happen, however, we can reach a point of readiness that is just as comparable. The growing will never stop until we die and become perfect, but we **CAN** be ready and waiting.

I ask myself often, *"Am I ready for my husband to meet me? Am I really ready? Am I at a place with God where my heart is full and content? Am I ready to take care of another person, share my heart with another person?"* Ask yourself some of your own tough questions, and quit bellyaching to every girl at church about your loneliness.

Today is the beginning of the end of your idiotic social media rants on how you are **#foreveralone**. That's not the type of childlike behavior God was referring to when He told us he wanted us to *"become as little children"*. When we are no longer enslaved by this type of immaturity, we will begin to believe that God created someone for us to enjoy; and enjoy we shall - because we will wait on the one who is worthy.

The Comeback Virgin

*. . .**B**ecause you really can, come back that is. As long as you call on the one who can pick you up and get you back on track, JESUS. It does not matter how far you have gone in the wrong direction or how many times you have tried to do the right thing and have fallen. The Bible says that a righteous man falls seven times (seven meaning completeness, often, many) but gets back up. Being righteous has nothing to do with falling. God calls you righteous when you can get back up!*

For a righteous man falleth seven times, and riseth up again; but the wicked are overthrown by calamity. Prov 24:16

Jesus left Heaven and came to the Earth as an ordinary man, so that we could live in eternity beside Him. He came to eliminate the bondage our sin keeps us in. He didn't sacrifice His body so that we could live like reckless whores under the covering of His grace. He came so that we could become free from our perverted ways. No matter what has happened you can live pure. The grace of God is waiting to restore you. The pain of your past can no longer hold you when you discover the grace of God. The hurt that others have put you through can no longer haunt you. He has come to deliver you. It's crazy to think about....really. To think that God knew you were going to fall when He decided to love you. Knowing about all your mess-ups and disturbances, He decided to go for it, to die for you! He decided your destiny was far more important than all your flaws and mistakes. He believes in you more than you can even imagine, and if you let Him work within you, He will do far more than you could ever ask or imagine! We can't do it on our own, but with His power at work within us, neither penis nor temptation can stand in our way.

If we confess our sins, he is faithful and just and will forgive us our sins and purify us from all unrighteousness. 1 John 1:9

Repent, then, and turn to God, so that your sins may be wiped out, that times of refreshing may come from the Lord. Acts 3:19

He knows your potential, and is doing everything He possibly can to get you to the great things He has for you. You have to let go of your agenda and trust Him. Accept His grace and let Jesus help you live in purity.

Now to him who is able to do immeasurably more than all we ask or imagine, according to his power that is at work within us.

Eph 3:20

LISA

...The "Try Again" Virgin

I recently made a huge decision to move to the surprisingly rad hipster city of Minneapolis, MN to take a position in ministry at a thriving church. I'm not going to lie to you, this being hometown to the legendary rock star Prince, helped me out in the decision making process... *"RIP Prince"*.

When I first met all the people that were on my new team, in this new position I had taken on, Lisa most definitely stood out to me the most. To be honest, at first, she was a bit intimidating. She was bold, confident, and knew exactly what she wanted and needed. I could tell right away she was not to be messed with, and that she probably thought I was a bit too young to be taking on this job. I could be wrong, but I'm probably not. Lisa is a beautiful African American woman with curves and curls. She's well put together and brilliant; quiet at first, but talkative when she feels comfortable with you. We were meeting about her specific area on the team, when I discovered her crazy story about her virginity.

Lisa didn't grow up in church and was never specifically encouraged to save herself for marriage. Nevertheless, she held out until the age of 20 to cash in her V card for a guy she now refers to as Mr. 1 Minute Man. *(These are the type of stories that terrify me about having sex.)* Basically, she hated her first sex experince! He put it in and took it right out and boom her virginity was gone. After a week of having 1-minute sex with *"Mr. Can't Keep It In"*, he

VICTORIA RAE' RICH

disappeared and she never heard from him again. Lisa went into a deep depression. She cried all hours of the night and couldn't figure out why she couldn't *get ok*. Weeks went by, and she wasn't eating nor was she sleeping. She didn't even realize how bad the situation was until one day she passed out. Within a month's time, Lisa had lost 30 lbs. It took a year for her to be alright again. It's insane to me how one decision can mess us up for years. 60 seconds of sex can wreck us for a lifetime. The world doesn't want us to make a big deal out of sex, but Lisa's story tells us otherwise!

A year went by without Mr. 1 Minute Man, and Lisa was starting to feel like her old self again, except this time around she was angry. Angry at men. Angry at life, and ready to treat men the way she had been treated. A free meal and movie was all she cared about now. Screw men and love; just give me the free food, dude! She felt used and abused, and she didn't have the energy to care about anyone else's feelings but her own. This was the beginning of a lot of men she would use in the years to come.

Clubs consumed her life. One night in particular she thought to herself, *"I'm going to have a one night stand! I've never had one and it's time for me to try it out!"* ... So she did. She met a guy at the club and took him home. We will refer to this guy as **Mini Slim Jim.** Lisa: (her own words) *"His D was so small it was a waste of a one night stand. The joke, 'Is it in yet?' came to mind. Of course, he thought he was doing big things... but NOPE."* After the horrible sex, Lisa told him he had to go *(which is so like her to say)* and that she had to work early the next morning *(LIE)*. Of course he wanted to stay… *(I mean where else is Mr. Slim Jim going to go)*. So, she allowed this stranger to stay.

This guy instantly became a stage 5 clinger and wouldn't leave her alone. He begged her to go on dates with him and just give him a chance. So because of the free movie and dinner, she agreed to a date. She was getting attention at least, and that was all that mattered. After date #3 he asked her to come back to his place *(for some more little Slim Jim sex)*. They were sitting on his bed getting ready to get their 'Netflix and Chill' on when a female walks into the room and screams, *"Do you know who I am?!"* Lisa looked at her stunned and smarted off with: *"Uh, he told me you were his roommate."* She instantly knew that wasn't the right thing to say when the girl becomes infuriated and yells at Slim, *"I'm the roommate now?!"* The two girls just looked at him as he stared off into space. This girl now begins to fight Slim and hits him in the face! Lisa grabbed her purse and jetted out of there! Turns out, that young lady was his fiancé and Slim made her keep her things in another bedroom so he could cheat on her. This chick started texting and calling poor Lisa explaining her struggles with him, and they actually became good friends! (Imagine that) Lisa said she felt like she was in a movie. She couldn't believe this was real life. So here she is once again, alone and upset with her decisions, but the story wasn't over yet.

Little Slim Jim had come and gone, but a bigger problem had arisen for Lisa. Lisa had known this new problem (aka man) throughout high school and knew he had a thing for her. "So, why not use him?!" she asked herself. **Enter Magnum.** *(as she called him)* He quickly became the guy she turned to when she needed a release, if you know what I'm saying. "No one needed to know about this!" she screamed to herself. This was not the guy she would ever think about bringing around mom and dad, and he was the complete opposite of Slim. Quickly, she became addicted to him. Infatuated with him. Even though she knew she shouldn't be with him, she made an exception because her body needed him. Magnum was a drug dealer. Yep, the type of guy that hid pills in his teeth to sell on the street. Lisa had gone too far. The 20 year old virgin, who was depressed for a year about giving it up to someone who threw her away, was now an attention craving, club banger, who had nasty wild sex with a teeth rotting drug dealer on the weekly.

I know all too well that he may make your body feel very good, but in reality he is killing your spirit, your dreams, your ambitions and your morality. It's not his fault. It's yours.

Lisa started going to church, and God began to talk to her about her lifestyle. Without anyone telling her she needed to stop having sex, she started to feel the pull to change on her own. She broke up with her boyfriend at the time and made a vow to God to keep herself until marriage. I absolutely loved hearing Lisa's story, because she was truly at the lowest point in her little slutty ways, and Jesus turned her life completely around. She's been sex free for 4 years and is currently waiting on the man God has for her.

… Where the Spirit of the Lord is, there is freedom. And we all, who with unveiled faces reflect the Lord's glory, are being transformed into His image with ever-increasing glory, which comes from the Lord. 2 Corinthians 3:17-18

Trust in the Lord with all your heart and lean not on your own understanding; in all your ways submit to Him, and He will make your paths straight. Proverbs 3:5-611

Confidence, Class, Charisma

Confidence:

I have fallen for guys before just because they were so confident! **PAUSE:** Can I tell you a quick story? There was this guy in college that just thought he was God's gift to the female race, and to be honest with you, he was kind of ugly! He was an incredible musician, which was attractive, yet it still wasn't good enough to accommodate for his bad looks. However, because of his incredible confidence I fell for him...hard! He made me believe that I wanted him, and I eventually did! He was charming. He believed in himself, and in return I believed in him. It's amazing where you can get in life when you simply believe you can get there.

How can we believe in ourselves, when others have torn down our confidence with negative words? Let God have the last say about you. You are HIS daughter. He made you perfectly for what He has for you to do on this Earth. No one else can say jack about you. **YOU ARE HIS!**

I knew you before I formed you in your mother's womb. Before you were born I set you apart...

Jeremiah 1:5

How beautiful you are and how pleasing, O love, with your delights!

Song of Solomon 7:6

3 Keys to finding and sustaining your confidence:

1. Know your unique significance

What is it that you have that no one else on Earth possesses? What has He put you on this Earth to do? Let Him reveal it to you. There is no way possible you can't be confident when you know your significance.

2. Don't let people tear you down

Take out the trash, and leave it in the can! Don't go diggin' back in it when you get bored or lonely.

People are like elevators: they will either take you up or bring you down. If you are surrounding yourself with people who are only bringing you down, then you can't ever expect to go up. Don't date guys who don't see your worth! If they view you as trash, then that's exactly what they are. Get rid of them! If they only want you for what you're carrying on your back or chest, get rid of them!

Those things are gonna sag one day, and unfortunately he will be gone before they start hangin' low!

3. Trust God

No matter what you may be going through, trust that God knows what He's doing.... And to be quite honest, He does! You might be waiting 5 more years on the man God has for you and that messes with our confidence sometimes. Honestly, the fact that I'm 26, and I'm not in any kind of relationship at all, *(while watching all my friends fall in love, get married, and have children)* has injured my confidence at times. However, you can't allow yourself to go to that place. There is a reason you're going through all that you are going through. Stay strong and confident that God will finish what He started in you and for you. *I consider it a privilege to WAIT on God... if this is the one thing I get to give to Him, what an honor that is! Lord, I want my life to be a living sacrifice offered ONLY to you.*

Freckles, thick glasses, pom-poms, polos... Tight skirt, cleavage, long locks... none of these things truly have anything to do with being sexy or confident. *Being sexy and confident has everything to do with you being comfortable in your own skin.* Knowing who you are as a woman and living that out to the fullest...that is sexy. *Confidence is the sexiest thing we could ever possess.* Confidence and deodorant of course; a toothbrush might be a good thing to invest in as well. (Ha!)

Class:

Just be ladylike. Burping the loudest to outdo your girlfriend is not going to get you a date with prince charming. If you haven't brushed your teeth in a week, I promise you, unless he's a complete whack job, he's not going to enjoy digging the thick yellow gunk out of your teeth with his tongue.

Don't expect to be treated like a lady, if you don't act like one. If you act like a floozy, you'll find yourself with a real man whore. If you act like a lady, a gentleman will come along. *You can't let every dog on the block bury their bone in your garden.* **Keep that garden fresh and clean!**

Have standards. Don't settle for anything less than you deserve. Believe you deserve the very best, then start acting like you do.

A woman with class knows what she wants and doesn't settle for anything less. A woman with class doesn't have to take her clothes off to get noticed. She walks into a room, and every guy notices her presence. The trash is thrown out when the class walks in.

Don't give in to social pressures like: Kissing other girls, getting wasted at the party, or white girl twerking upside down on the wall. That kind of behavior may get his attention for the night, but if he has any decency at all; he won't take you home to meet his parents. Don't expect him to drop a significant amount of money for a rock on your left hand either, because to him you aren't by any means showing that you are worth the sacrifice and work he has to put in to get you that ring. He would rather just watch you get wasted, then bang you, and forget it happened until the next time he's horny. **CLASS** ladies; get some....please!

Charisma:

Charisma will come naturally when you have confidence. They go hand in hand. Bury yourself in Jesus, and the confidence will come. Your charisma won't look like anyone else's, so quit trying to be like anyone other than yourself; it will never work. Quit waiting to turn into Sally, you were made a Jane; it's not going to happen! Explore your personality, and live it out to the fullest. Whatever that may look like for you. Once you find your unique charisma, don't let anyone take that from you. It doesn't matter how much they don't like it, it's not their place to give an opinion about who God has created you to be. *(Unless they are your spiritual leader and you just be actin' a crazy fool...insert disappointed face)* I'm not saying you don't need to take correction when you act like a crazy person, rather what I'm saying is: Don't let people tear your confidence down or try to take away your God given personality and character traits.

RAINA

...The Fool In Love
*"I'm going to find you and blow your brains out, b****!"*
Two days later, "I love you so much Raina. I promise I'll be

different!" This is the endless game that young, insecure
Raina will have to go through for years until she finds
the strength to put a stop to it. Raina was 16 years old
when Jacob walked up to her all smooth like butter, telling her how beautiful she was. He was tall, dark, handsome, and a bit of a bad boy, which Raina found sexy
and appealing. She usually fell for the bad boy type. I
recently interviewed Raina and asked her to explain to
me exactly what went down with this psycho trip. She
told me: at first, she didn't realize he was a lunatic until
things began to become more serious. When sex started
to become a regular thing, he began to show her his true
colors. Anger, bad language, drugs, jealousy... She was
completely trapped in his uncontrollable anger, but she
thought she loved him. That's what having sex without
God's permission will do to us. It will blind us completely to what is actually going on.

My pastor once told me that when you become intimate with someone, it's like smashing your face up
against a picture frame and trying to see if it's straight on
the wall. You can't differentiate if the frame is crooked
or straight because you are way too close to it. It is only
when you take a step back, you can really tell if the picture is crooked or not. It's the same with inappropriate
sexual behavior. Once you become so close to someone,
it's difficult to judge the reality of what is actually going
on.

Raina finally got away from Jacob after years of abuse.
I remember the time when she knew she'd had enough.
She woke

up and decided she was better than what he was putting her through, and he wasn't the only man on the planet for goodness sake! She knew God had better for her! She deserved to be treated with respect and honor. No way was she going to repeat the pattern of behavior her mother had to endure as a young woman! God restored her confidence and washed her clean. Raina is now promised to be married to a wonderful man who treats her like the incredible woman that she is and I couldn't be more proud of them both.

Quit running the Good Guys off

Advice on picking up the **RIGHT** guys, and what the heck, any guy for that matter. Because, let's face it, if you are picking up the right guys; you are most likely to pick up the wrong ones as well. There are a few keys to picking up men that I want to share with you. It's a proven fact, men are more likely to be attracted to you - when you convey **confidence,** and less likely if you are **insecure**. It's not just about looking the hottest. We all have flaws, but we can't dwell on them or pick ourselves apart day after day. Get out of the mirror!

Your outward flaws will be beautiful to the heart that is meant to have yours.

Your awkwardness will fit perfectly with the awkwardness of the heart that is supposed to possess yours. Be confident in knowing that God has created you just the way you are, and that He will not leave you alone.

Trust that He has made someone to fit perfectly with the person you already are, flaws and all. When you are confident, no matter what is wrong with you physically or mentally, you will not only attract the opposite sex; but also people in general. People all over the world are looking and waiting for someone to stand up with complete confidence, and lead them in a positive direction. The people of this world need a leader. That leader is you! Just believe in yourself, everything is possible with God! Let nothing stand in your way! Especially your negative thoughts and emotions about yourself.

A few pointers:

1. Brush your teeth at least twice daily. No one likes stanky breath. *(unless they themselves are stankin'...then y'all can stank together.)*

2. Explore beauty tips *(use the internet)*. Stay on top of the latest trends. Learn how to do your makeup, girl! Master that bun! Ain't nothing wrong with lookin' good!

3. Wear clothes that flatter your figure. Don't try to fit into something you can't pull off. Don't let your belly hang over your jeans. Start working out. Your health is extremely important.

4. Don't be a stage 5 clinger. Don't call him more than once a day *(if that)* until you know he loves you. Let him

be the one to pursue you. Men should always be the one doing the pursuing! The Bible says, *"HE who finds a wife finds a GOOD thing..." Prov. 18:22*

5. No smothering. Absence makes the heart grow fonder. Why do you think Jesus left for a period of time? *"...I go to prepare a place for you, I will come again..." John 14:3* Come quickly, Lord Jesus.

6. Don't become desperate. If you are indeed "thirsty", don't let him see it!

7. Don't fall in love on the first date *(and if you do just keep it to yourself for awhile until he conveys the same interest)*

"Above all else, guard your heart..." Prov. 4:23

8. Don't nag him. *(If you don't like who he is, you shouldn't be dating him in the first place)*

9. Have standards. *(Don't let him do whatever he wants to your body)* 'A man wants your skirt long enough to cover the essentials and short enough to create interest.' I heard a preacher say that once before.

10. Classy is key *(All men like a gal with some class; don't burp or pass gas)*

*Don't show him all your tricks on the first hand. Play

hard to get, guys go crazy over that stuff! Make him work for you. If he's not willing to work for you, then he's just not that into you.

One thing that will help you attract the right men in your life, is being confident in your principles. When a woman can stand up for what she believes in, and never allow herself to be pulled to the right or left. When she can stand firmly on what she knows deep down in her heart is right and true, that is **sexy**! Trust me, men will agree. I have had a 100% success rate with laying down the law with anyone I have ever dated...and I haven't dated the best of men at times, but I always stayed true to who I was. That doesn't mean I was perfect, but there was a line I set in my heart that I wasn't going to cross. I never had a guy to make fun of me or dump me for not wanting to have sex with them...not a single one. Doesn't mean they wouldn't try at times or ask many times. After all, they are still men, ladies. They are going to try. At the end of the day, they admired and respected what I stand for. The majority of the guys I've dated, I feel, possibly fell in love with me only because of Jesus in me. *(My perfected bun probably helped as well...)*

I have to rant for a minute. (of course I do, *rolls eyes*)

Bare with me will you? I am typically around A LOT of single Christian women who CONSTANTLY talk about how badly they are in need of the perfect guy. Or how they feel their wombs are drying up, and how their chances of reproduction are slim and so on.... *(I'm exaggerating, just a little bit)* Anyway, it irks me because we are supposed to be examples of strength, not perfection.

Solid strength. We lean on the ROCK. We are the women who have Jesus, the savior of the universe. He listens to our prayers. He counts the hairs on our head and waits for the day He can receive us in Heaven. We have found our purpose in the one who has conquered death and the grave. Yet, here we are scared senseless that we will never find a human man to call a husband! Quit belly-aching about your doubt, because that's what you're really doing! Quit talking to everybody about how there aren't any good men anywhere! That's unattractive and faithless. God didn't mess up and forget to create your husband! Guys hear that kind of crap from a mile away anyway and are immediately turned off! Get your faith back! God is in control and knows what He's doing.

Indeed, the very hairs of your head are all numbered. Don't be afraid... Luke 12:7

He is not going to bring someone else into the mix, until your relationship with Him is pouring out a sweet savor of good vibes! He is a jealous God and will put His relationship with you above all else, even your own emotions.

...For the Lord, whose very name is jealous, is a God who is jealous about his relationship with you. Exodus 34:14

Now, listen, you can add a random dude to the equation that has no reason for being in your life, but if you do that; you will continue to go around in circles like you're on a nightmare of a merry go round. **Chill out**.

Quit yammering to every church girl you meet. Talk to God, that's what He's waiting on. TRUST HIM.

Live out your destiny while you wait.

I have a fellow "PK" (Preacher's kid) friend who is bossing it out in her father's church in Illinois. She does everything from: leading the worship department to running the children's and teens departments in her thriving family church. I first met Liz during a collaboration of creative leaders, who had come together to strategize and plan messages for their teen ministries. She inspired me greatly. Here was a young single woman who was practically running her father's church with such tenacity and strength. She was truly living out her destiny while she waited. What a great example she was to me. I'm sure at times she became lonely. I'm sure at times it became hard on her, but I never once heard her complain or doubt God. I didn't even hear her whine or become angry with God. I only heard her speak with such faith in God and how she knew without a doubt, He was going to take care of her. I recently got a call from Liz, who is now a 37 yr old virgin! (and I think I've waited a long time, get it Liz!) She was calling to invite me to her wedding. We giggled and laughed like little girls in awe of what God had done in her life.

Never lose sight of what God has called you to do. Work hard and be diligent, and in God's perfect timing He will take care of all of your heart desires.

Take delight in the Lord, and He will give you the desires of your heart. Psalm 37:4

(and in case you were wondering... her fiancé is fine! He's gifted and working right alongside her in ministry. He's absolutely hilarious with a fantastic personality. This guy is always encouraging Liz as she follows the heart of God. Watch out now! GO FORTH AND MULTIPLY LIZZY!)

TALK 8

Your behavior = No Ring

Ladies, you **DO NOT** have to take off your clothes, have sex, or suck a D, to receive the kind of love you are waiting for. Don't be afraid to tell him what you will **NOT** do! Ignore the ignorant rap songs about the big booty bad hoes.

Should we wear tiny shorts with our butt cheeks hanging out so all the boys will say *"hey girl heyyyy!"* Or pick out the tightest thing we can get our hands on to show off our ta tas?! **NO!** Men are most definitely visual creatures and they will look at you and drool over you if you show off everything you've got. That kind of man will also treat you like a piece of meat, and throw you out as soon as they are finished with you. You wonder why all the men you deal with are dogs... Well, maybe it's because you keep letting them bury their bones in your yard. *(clearing my throat)* Let me say this, men aren't the only ones who can be sexual monsters. Women, you are just as brazen, but we will get to that later, you little freaks...

Girls, if you show them everything you have on the first date... wait, let me backup a little bit. If you are showing them everything you have before they even ask you on a date, the kind of men you are going to attract are going to be the ones who only want you for your big ta-tas and tight butt cheeks. Why would a good man ever marry a trashy slut? Guess what? They won't. It's never too late to change however. Thank God for His grace and incredible love that covers and cleans us up no matter how filthy we are. Unfortunately, we are all filthy until Jesus invades our lives. We don't deserve His grace, but He allows us to enjoy it anyway.

Wash me clean from my guilt. Purify me from my sin. Psalm 51:2

My grace is sufficient for you, for my power is made perfect in weakness. 2 Corinthians 12:9

Yes, I'm that virgin chick that always says no to the guys who only want sex, and wait for the guy who is willing to wait for me. Most times, I've thought, I would probably lose a guy if I told Him where I stood with sex, but every one of those times I was wrong. Every time I was honest with them, they appreciated how I respected my body and my future. It was then they wanted to be a part of my future, because they knew it was going to be special.

In my experience, it has been devilishly difficult to find a guy I am attracted to, that is seeking after God in the same ways I am. At 26 years old, it's starting to feel like a long wait. Yes, some of you might be older than I am, call me names, go ahead, but in my opinion it does not matter the age, the feeling still remains true. It is lonely waiting on the man God has designed for you.

The waiting sucks. I know some of you, who are reading this, may have a very confused look on your face and are probably screaming; *"Ummm excuse me virgin girl, I found my man of God at 18 years old and we already have two babies!"* To you, I say congrats, but there are millions of us who are waiting patiently. I'm not a very patient person when it comes to my personal life. I like to succeed, get the goods now! This character trait has been hard to tame while waiting on my husband. I have kissed many horny toads waiting on my beloved God fearing prince, and I'm not gonna lie, many times I have been tempted as well. Causing myself to fall into the trap of the famous *"make out sessions gone wrong, way wrong."* But after all of that, I have realized the sexiest thing I could ever do to a guy is tell him he can't have my goods. I'm telling you girls, they go crazy for it! Whether they admit it or not, they will love you for not giving in to their D. Once they can respect you, they will love you. When lust is out of the way, there is room for true love. Love that will last. Love that will put a ring on your finger. (*not just knock you up*) It requires patience, self-discipline, and a lot of **Jesus**! But I promise you, your future husband will find it the sexiest thing he has ever experienced. **You will stand out** and he will appreciate it. Test it and see.

Love is patient. Love is kind. It does not dishonor others, it is not proud.

I Corinthians 13:4

Let me remind you again, your behavior = no ring.

Why are you so thirsty?!

He doesn't have to put the ring on your finger, because you are already treating him as if he is your husband. Have you ever noticed those couples that have been together for about 7 1/2 years, and he still hasn't proposed? First question, are they living together? Second question, are they sleeping together? *(and no, I don't mean naps.)* I'm talking about sex. Third question, do they have children together? If any of these answers were yes (and are true in your case as well) then DUH, why would he want to spend a few grand on a ring and go through the trouble of a wedding, if you are already dishing out your wifely duties?

HE'S COMFORTABLE! Shake that boy up! Quit dishing out your private parts to a man that isn't your husband! He needs to want you! He needs to wake up and realize the amazing woman you are! Rewind and take back your best parts from him. **Quit acting like a wife, when he hasn't made any moves to make you one!**

I went to church with a couple that had been living together for around 8 years. They did everything together, yet their relationship was very unhealthy. Their intense fights would go on for days, sometimes weeks. She remained confused and distraught at the fact that he would not marry her. It didn't make any sense to her. Here she was giving up her entire life for him, and he wasn't doing the one thing she always wanted. She wanted the ring.

She wanted a family. The solidity of knowing he wanted her forever is all she asked for, yet he refused. I watched them go around in circles for years. I saw them take break after break. I kept quiet as she began to flirt with other men, invite them over to her place late at night, and try to sway them to have sex with her. She did this to one of my closest guy friends. It saddened me to watch them waste so many years of their lives. Years they could have had children. Years they could have lived in peace under God's blessings.

Unless He is a man after God's heart and is feeling guilty about not being your husband, (*while having crazy wild sex with you*) then you will probably need to start begging now, in order to get that ring and get the job done. I don't know about you, but I want my man to want to put that rock on my finger. There will be **NO** begging on my part. You have to give your man something to look forward to. You have to keep him guessing, wondering. Don't let him get near your cookies. Save those cookies for the appropriate timing. **Quit ruining the dinner by dishing out the dessert!** Put a lock on that cookie jar and throw away the key until your glorious wedding night! *AS SOON AS YOU MAKE THAT COVENANT YOU CAN SMASH THE COOKIE JAR ON THE GROUND AND LET THOSE COOKIES LOOSE!*

TALK 9
CRAVE Sex?

"Everything is permissible for me, but not everything is beneficial. 'Everything is permissible for me' – but I will not be mastered by anything." 1 Corinthians 6:12

*A**re you addicted already?* Are you having trouble kicking sexual habits? Once you start, it's like any other addiction…. you crave it. It takes over your thoughts. It becomes your master. You turn into a slave to whatever it is you are feeding. Is it the first thing you think about when you wake up and the last thing that runs through your mind before you fall asleep? If so, whatever it is has become your idol now. Satan wants your mornings and evenings committed to him. It's extremely hard to let go of sexual habits, because God created sex for a man and his wife to spiritually become one. However, it's certainly not hopeless for you, and you are not alone!

One way to kick this habit is to surround yourself with positive people, who are going to push you in the right direction. If you're addicted to any type of sexual activity, whether that be pornography or the actual act itself, don't surround yourself with people/person that tempts you. It's difficult to say no, especially if he pressures you. It's like putting a talking bag of weed in front of a pot head for hours on end, *"Just one last time baby…"* Surrounding yourself with friends who brag about their sexual relationships are only going to make you think it's alright to go ahead and act the way they do. Get real with them. Be the strong incredible woman of God you are, and encourage your floozy girlfriends to **want to wait.** *(Buy them a copy of this book ;))* Give them examples of how to really make the guy they are with, want them more than they have ever wanted them, by making them WAIT! **Set the new sexy trend, Good Girl!** Once again, I say this with experience. There were many times in my life, when I had to cut sexual habits and it was not easy. I'd created idols in my life without even knowing it. Even if it was simply just being consumed by a crush. But I have also experienced freedom from those habits and you can as well. *Masturbation, pornography, foreplay, oral sex, sexting--* all of these can become bondage *(not the sexy kind of bondage)* to our souls. The good news is we don't have to stay enslaved to sin. It's possible ladies, to live a pure life no matter what you have done. Jesus wants you clean, and He is willing to come where you are to get you back to where you're supposed to be with Him.

Let's go a little deeper into the many things that we can be tempted by and how important it is to be disciplined enough to keep our bodies in check.

"Flee from sexual immorality. All other sins a person commits are outside the body, but whoever sins sexually, sins against their own body."

I Corinthians 6:18

HORNY?

If simply being horny is the issue, I feel you, Good Girl. In my experience, the more I am exposed to the burning sensation the more I want it. You usually won't have cravings for things you've never experienced before. You are either exposing yourself to sexually explicit websites, music, movies, or the real life stuff. If you want to truly clean up your life, and begin to live pure you have to clean everything out. It all starts with your mouth. What goes in your mouth and what comes out of it, is far more important that you would have ever imagined!

TIGHT REIGN ON THE TONGUE

His D isn't a toothpick; get it out of your mouth. Tame the tongue, and clean your mouth out with the Word of God.

I'm being funny, but in all seriousness, to make this very simple, keep your tongues in your mouths. When that little tongue escapes and gets out of control, you are screwed. The only thing that needs to be ON YOUR TONGUE is the word of God.

Those who consider themselves religious and yet do not keep a tight rein on their tongues deceive themselves, and their religion is worthless.

James 1:26

"The Spirit of the Lord spoke through me; his word was on my tongue."

2 Samuel 23:2

What's been on your tongue lately? You will probably NEVER hear someone use these scriptures in this context (haha). God really cares about what we say and how we say it. He created everything you see with His words. Your future and destiny can be dictated by what comes out of your mouth. So I'm here to say: watch what comes out of your mouth! Don't allow it to be negative words and also, don't allow it to be someone's D, or somebody's nasty tongue!

I've done a lot of French kissing in my day, I'm not going to lie to you. But to be real, it's probably not a very good thing to allow yourself to get carried away with. Let's think about it, if you feel comfortable enough with someone to lick, suck, and bite on their tongue, taking your clothes off isn't that big of a deal right? *(Ha!)*

James 3 talks about how the tiny tongue can control the whole body. Isn't it weird how most sexual acts begin with a little tongue action? Once the tongue has done all it can do, then the body takes over and gets out of control. That tongue will start a fire that can't be put out. I used to think there was nothing wrong with making out, until I fell hard for someone and tongue action wasn't enough, I wanted *IT ALL!* If we can tame our tongue, we can tame our body. The same goes for your words as well. You are controlled by what you say.

Out of the mouth the heart speaks. (Luke 6:45)

James 3:3 When we put bits into the mouths of horses to make them obey us, we can turn the whole animal. 4 Or take ships as an example. Although they are so large and are driven by strong winds, they are steered by a very small rudder wherever the pilot wants to go. 5 Likewise, the tongue is a small part of the body, but it makes great boasts. Consider what a great forest is set on fire by a small spark. 6 The tongue also is a fire, a world of evil among the parts of the body. It corrupts the whole body, sets the whole course of one's life on fire, and is itself set on fire by hell.

Texting counts as *"talking"* by the way. If you're sexting someone, most likely that will lead to sending them a few nudes... Then that will probably lead to meeting up in person. Dirty talk is not ok. Role playing and pretending certain sexual things are happening through texting is not okay. You're speaking those things that are not as though they were, and eventually they will become real! That's how it works. You can speak things into existence, good or bad! That's how God designed it. He created the entire universe with His words. *(Gen 1:2)* If you simulate nasty situations with your words, it's as if you were actually doing those things in real time. When you lust in your heart, you might as well have done the act. *(But I tell you that anyone who looks at a woman lustfully has already committed adultery with her in his heart. Matthew 5:27)* I know because I've done it. I've pretty much tried everything to keep myself from actually *"doing it."* I became addicted to talking to someone. He was far away, "No one would know…." I told myself. "I could talk to him however I wanted, nothing wrong with it." **NOPE! I WAS WRONG!** It's not ok for your fear of loneliness to be the excuse as to why you waste your time and someone else's. I had myself messed up for a long time! Lust can control your mind and even your heart. It can make your emotions go wild and even blind you to what is actually happening around you. Lust can make you talk to someone for years without ever seeing them in person! Lust will cause your feelings to lie to you and make you think you feel a certain way. I know this, because it happened to me. **God wants our full attention. NO MORE IDOLS! Put Jesus in His proper place.**

"Delight yourself also in the LORD: and he shall give you the desires of your heart." Psalm 37:4

He wants our imagination and expectation. He wants to take it and make our dreams bigger and better than we ever thought they could be. He can't do all that He desires to do with our lives, if we hold tight to sin! Our eyes can not look at evil and Jesus at the same time. We have to let go of everything that separates us from Jesus so that He can set us free from everything and anything we've ever been bound by. He can take our broken hearts, lustful thoughts, and sexual addictions and in return allow our wildest dreams to come true. He wants to exchange our tears for joy. He wants to hold us when we feel lonely. He wants to wash us clean when we are neck deep in sexual guilt. All we have to do is simply let go of the trash so that He can give us all it is that we need.

When we make ourselves pure before God there is nothing we can't have, do, or be.

HE rewards well.

If we can FIRST above all else, control our tongues, we will be able to control our bodies. Once you can master when to stop kissing, you won't have any trouble keeping your hands to yourself. Taking your clothes off won't even be a thought that crosses your mind once you are able to keep your mouth in line. Tame your tongue and temptation won't overthrow you.

Tame the tongue.

Control the mind.

Guard your heart.

Don't be swayed by emotions.

Don't give up on the wait.

CUT out all filthy music. I know it has a nice beat and all of that, but it's not helping you wait for the right man, I promise it's not. How do you expect to have pure thoughts throughout the day, when the first thing you're feeding your mind with in the morning is a filthy explicit song about sex? You may not realize how much of an effect music is actually having on you, until you begin to feed your spirit with something edifying to God. I've noticed when I'm in a horrible mood, and I turn on music that is worshiping God it will immediately change the course of my day. I'll become happy and uplifted because it's feeding my soul and spirit! It's the same with your bodies craving for sex. If you are jamming to filthy music, it will only increase your willingness to fall for the nasty guy, who wants to touch you in places only you should know about. Find music you love that doesn't make you want to slide down the stripper pole or grind on the first guy that walks by.

Do not conform to the pattern of this world, but be transformed by the renewing of your mind. Then you will be able to test and approve what God's will is--his good, pleasing and perfect will. Romans 12:2

GATES TO YOUR SOUL

It's not normal to watch PORN! Quit believing that lie.

The Bible teaches us that our eyes are gates to our souls. *The eye is the lamp of the body. So, if your eye is healthy, your whole body will be full of light. Matthew 6:22* When we watch impure videos it messes with our minds and fogs our vision, it replays in our heads provoking us to have impure thoughts at random times. It's uncontrollable. Porn can become just as addictive as any drug. There are demons and spirits that attach themselves to you when you open up that gate to your soul. You are welcoming demonic spirits into your spirit when you purposely watch those filthy sexual acts. What's funny is this: as I sat down to write today in the local bookstore, a Playgirl magazine was lying on the table right beside me! I left it there to remind me while I write, how hard it is to stay pure in such a filthy world. Sex is everywhere. Our television shows are just as bad as soft porn! Seriously, if you have watched any dramas on premium networks like HBO or Showtime, you have practically watched porn. How do I know this you ask? Because I've seen some of these shows and I know from experience they mess with your mind and prompt you to crave the very thing you are watching. It's dangerous. The filth and guilt I felt after watching these shows was not worth it! Don't give in! Watch something a little more respectful!

"You have heard that it was said, 'Do not commit adultery.' But I tell you that anyone who has looked at a woman lustfully has already committed adultery with her in his heart."
Matthew 5:28

If your eyes are filled with filth, your vision will not be clear for your life or your destiny. You can't see in faith if your vision is clogged. The enemy will do everything in his power to take your eyes off Jesus, because he knows as long as your eyes are on Him you will not sink. Peter was the only other man in the Bible that walked on water besides Jesus. It was only when he began to look around at the storm and waves, instead of on Jesus, that he began to sink. However, as soon as he began to sink,

Jesus reached out and grabbed Him and pulled him to safety. It's ok if your eyes are off the goal for a moment, as long as you get them back on what matters the most... Jesus. His love is never absent and is always faithful to pick us up.

"The eye is the lamp of the body. If your eyes are healthy, your whole body will be full of light. Matthew 6:22

During the last part of my college years I started to become very curious about sex. One of my Chrisitan mentors encouraged me to watch porn. Yes, you heard that right. One of my male Christian mentors found out I was a virgin and told me I should study porn so I would know how to please a man. Of course, I knew he was wrong and disgusting for saying these things to me, but for some reason it tempted me even more to explore. It was as if a demonic sexual spirit had attached itself to me and began to tell me it was just innocent curiosity. I began to watch porn, and for years had to struggle to get away from what became an addiction. DO NOT MESS WITH PORN! It's a strong demonic tool that Satan uses to trap us in, and it is not easy to break away from.

<u>Porn is murdering your imagination and your future sex life. Stop watching it.</u>

V CARD TRASHED

W hy are girls having sex so young? Are we not receiving the kind of love we need to survive? Pregnant teenagers and STD's are the norm in the world we live in. Why do we crave it so badly? Is it because we feel unloved? Is it because we are the fatherless generation? Is it because we have lost our purpose? Is it because sex is sold all over everything? WHAT IS IT about you that makes you crave sex/attention from the opposite sex so badly? Look deep inside yourself. Insecurities maybe? They can enable us to crave crazy things. Do you have a fear of being unloved? Does sex just feel too good? Rebellious maybe? Your dream is to live out a rap song?

Will he like me more if I suck it?

A lot of times I feel like I want to do sexual things to make the guy I'm seeing happy, or make him want me more. I want him to think, *"Ohhhh, that girl is good at doing that."* Sometimes we just want to sexually please the guy, because we assume that's the only way we will be able to **keep him.** If this is currently your situation, then he is not the one for you. If he is only with you because he's getting a blowjob from you a few times a week, then he is not husband material. If you deny him sex and he disappears, he was never good enough in the first place. Also, LISTEN, Good Girl! Your desire to please the man was given to you by God FOR MARRIAGE. Don't let Satan lie to you and tell you, "You're the only one who thinks that way, you little nasty girl!" We all think this way. We were designed by God to please our husbands. We can't let that God given desire take over at the wrong time though. Just wait, Good Girls, just wait.

ELLE

...the girl who gave him everything and it still wasn't enough. (Jesus requires nothing from us)

Taxicabs fly past us like the end of the world is at hand and we only have 3 min to get to the space shuttle that will take all the humans to heaven! The Chicago air is crisp and cold as it passes through my nostrils, and this scarf around my head definitely screams I'm from the south. I've gotta make my way to the middle of this crowd, to get some kind of warmth for goodness sake! I feel my pocket vibrating. I look at my phone and notice it's one of my best friends, Elle. I'm not a big phone talker, but I pick up the call nonetheless. It's been awhile since I've heard her valley girl accent, so I pick up and suddenly hear my friend frantically crying uncontrollably. *(This was nothing new, sorry Elle, you're an emotional being, and that's OK)* Let me backup for a moment, and provide you with a little history on Elle. Elle and I met through our parents who have been lifelong friends. We have both been *"preacher's daughters"* since the moment we took our very first breath of air. We grew up hearing our Daddies preach Holy Ghost blazin' fire *(spoken with a southern accent)* from the squeaky pews of our small town little churches. Elle and I always connected on the belief that sex should be saved for marriage. We are both very passionate about that subject. *(back to the story)* She begins to tell me that she lost her virginity to this guy she thought she loved and he broke up with her a few days afterwards. She then began to tell me how depressed she was, and how she didn't think she would ever forgive herself. First of all, I wanted to beat the crap out of the guy that broke her heart! Second, I hated with everything in me, that she thought she couldn't forgive herself - and thirdly, I wanted to slap her face for giving away her virginity, to a boy she had only known for a few weeks. **C'MON!** My friend began to tell me the details of her sexual experience... and my dear reader... this is where I should probably stop typing for your sake. *(I know you are thinking, "dang it was totally about to get all "50 Shades of Grey" up in here...but no thanks.)*

I recently interviewed my friend Elle and asked, *"Why did you give it up in such a short amount of time after waiting so long?"* These were a few of her responses... *"Hmmm, it was my first "big" relationship, I thought, and honestly; the temptation of being in our own room and alone all the time, made it so much harder. Also, with him not being a Christian, he was rather pushy on the issue of sex. He said all the things I thought I wanted to hear. I truly believed that he was somehow infatuated with me. I thought there was no way he would do me wrong, because he wanted me so badly. Obviously, you always wonder what it will be like, and having someone there that you believe you might be with for a long time; or even forever didn't make it easy. It all came down to one thing though… him not being a Christian. He didn't have any morals or values, so it was not a smart decision."*

Let us fast-forward to a year later … Elle's life is still totally consumed with Mr. Whine Butt. It makes me want to shoot his big toe off. Here's a guy that took her virginity and immediately broke up with her. He is now playing games with her mind, emotions, and body. He keeps her wrapped around his finger, with no regard for her mor- als or feelings about losing what she held on to so dearly, and for so long. Time after time he draws her back in and throws her back out. He's completely consumed with himself.

Elle's family went through a horrific tragedy when her father had a seizure in the middle of a Wal-Mart parking lot one day. Her father's personality is completely gone. He can barely walk, talk, or function on his own. He lost oxygen to his brain for 12 minutes during this episode. He was an outstanding preacher and musician and within a matter of minutes, one seizure changed their family and their church forever. She hasn't had the easiest life, and yet this boy goes on about his life day in and day out, **ON HIS TIME.** Her time becomes his time. She longs for just a sec, a minute, an hour; anything she can get with him. He comes first to her no matter what's going on in her life. His calls will get an answer from her… whether she likes it or not, she can't help but put him first. She gave him something that wasn't meant for him. So here she is trapped in this weird relationship with him, because she gave away the only thing that connects two souls and makes them one. Be careful to whom you are linking yourself up with! It frustrates me to no end to see her so vulnerable and weak! It's pathetic and I would do anything to get her out of this ditch she's put herself in.

We put our souls at risk when we consume ourselves with anything and anyone that isn't Jesus.

What does your mind do when you are giving a blowjob or letting him "pick the pansies" from your garden? Studies have shown: while girls/women are in the midst of a sexual act, their mind literally makes them believe they are in love with the person they are sexually involved with. They can't think or feel for themselves. When sex gets a hold of your heart and mind it is uncontrollable. It will start to become what is most important in your life. It was meant to consume, to change you forever, but in the context of marriage! You weren't meant to be joined with someone you only dated for 6 months or 2 weeks. You really think you're in love, better yet, know this person? Honey, take a few steps back from the picture on the wall so that you can see clearly. *Is this the man you prayed for?*

All Things NEW

I hate when a speaker begins to talk about virginity, all of the people in the room, who were getting down and dirty with their pants off last weekend; feel like there isn't any hope for them to regain purity. Jesus' grace covers it all and even though it feels like you will never kick the habit, I promise you, with His strength, you can.

So if the son sets you free, you will be free indeed. John 8:36

And He who sits on the throne said, "Behold, I am making all things new " And He said, "Write, for these words are faithful and true."

Revelation 21:5

Start now - making your future something special. Start now - building your foundation for marriage. This begins when you're single. You have to live your life with your future husband in mind. We don't live reckless just because we haven't felt Jesus' face or physically touched his scarred hands. We live for Him knowing He is coming back to get us soon. The one who deserves your heart is on his way… start prepping now!

Have Faith

You don't care who uses your body, because you don't care about your future. You don't believe you will receive anything better than what you already have. It's a lie and a trick from hell to keep you away from what God has for you. You must have faith and trust in GOD. If you've never had a father and you are always seeking attention from men, come to THE FATHER who loves you the most! Get the Spiritual help you need! Your issues can be resolved…you can be fixed. You just have to make the decision to trust God and have faith.

Do not be afraid, little flock, for your Father has been pleased to give you the kingdom. Luke 12:32

Aye, little flock ladies, don't fear. We have God. We have one another. Somewhere out there is the man designed for us, and he is looking... He's looking.

Horny Feelings Lie

Y*our gut isn't always God. Feelings do not always = facts.*
Get rid of your thirsty, horny feelings.
  Are you hearing from God? No ma'am, that's called a mid-life crisis. Shut up and see what Jesus has to say. **Warning:** you may not like what He has to reveal about your unfaithful gigolo.
  Lucy is a 55 year old virgin. *I KNOW RIGHT?!* I thought I was waiting a long time! Recently she lost a significant amount of weight and feels *"confidence"* on a whole new level. *(confidence: key to attracting men)* She suddenly began to receive attention from men for the first time in her virgin life. It wasn't long before she fell into what she thought was love and went absolutely *CUCKOO. (Acting Cuckoo: the key to locking men out of your bedroom for the rest of your life.)*
  Clingy isn't even a strong enough word to describe what she turned into. This confident, funny, talented, classy woman, I have known all my life, was now on the phone with my mother balling her eyes out. All over a man who had no business in her bed in the first place! When I say she was balling, what I really mean is, her crying was like witnessing a torrential rainstorm.
  She has become completely obsessed. I used to look up to her, this fiery *Woman Preacher* who could make any

audience leave laughing in pure joy. I'm not judging her or blaming her in any way - for falling hard for this loser. I mean, I can't say I wouldn't have done the same thing if I were in her shoes. Fifty-Five years old and she wasn't receiving any action! Lord Jesus! What breaks my heart is that her ministry doesn't matter much to her anymore. Her relationship with God has all but flown out the window - well, minus the part where she believes He told her this man was *the one*!

Lucy literally doesn't care about much of anything, only pleasing this man. Cooking meals for him, whining and dining him. Cleaning his home when he and his wife are gone. Hoping he shows up to spend the night with her instead of going home to his wife where he belongs! She began giving up everything she has ever believed in, and this man has the nerve to poke fun at the fact, she is still a little overweight. He's a complete idiot, and this is who you believe Jesus is telling you to leave everything you've worked so hard for?

Excuse me, do you know how much Jesus loves you? He loves you so much, he would never cheat on you and never leave you on a date at *White Castle* for another woman. He would never call you ugly or fat. He would never trigger you to feel insecure. He would never take you away from your dreams, or drive you INSANE. He would never call you from his *wife's phone,* to tell you he's decided to stay with her tonight. I mean come on! How many times do we convince ourselves this is what God wants for me, when in reality this is really what *WE* want to do?

A *feeling* is not a word from God. We think because our emotions feel good, and because we've never experienced this type of feeling before, that it's from God. It doesn't help that music, television shows, books etc.... make us feel that if it feels right, then it must be right. Hear me out: I'm not saying every single time your feelings are going to mislead you. What I am saying is, just because you feel an extreme emotion for someone, does not mean *God* is speaking to you about them. You have to have another confirmation to solidify the feelings. The Bible says, *His word cuts us like a two edged sword*. I'm sure it didn't settle well with *Abraham's* heart, when God told him to sacrifice his own son's life at the altar. *YES*, God asked someone in the Bible to kill their own son. *(but an angel of God stopped him right before it happened)* Yet still, God asked that of him! I don't think that tickled Abraham's heart or gave him an overwhelming feeling of joy to hear those words, but it was still God's word. It was His voice speaking to him, and asking him to do this unspeakable act. Most of the time when God speaks to us, He's telling us to do things that we wouldn't normally want to do. Things we wouldn't necessarily think or do on our own. **He is constantly pushing us to our highest point of strength, while making us the best version of us we could possibly be.**

Lucy has encountered God's voice through friends, who are incredible individuals, with an awesome love of God. She simply will not listen to them. She doesn't want to face the reality of what God is asking of her, might hurt a little bit and might require much sacrifice on her part. It may just be the hardest thing she's ever had to do.

Why would God allow me to fall for someone at my age, then rip him away? Why does He allow me to continue to be hurt and broken-hearted? Why isn't God changing him and making him leave his wife? I'm sure she has asked herself these kinds of questions, but you know what, it's not God's fault.

Think about this:

1. She could have saved herself a lot of heartache, if she would have walked away once she found out he was still married.

2. *It IS NOT God's fault* she fell in love with a complete jerk. She failed the test placed in front of her. Wake up and get back on track if this story applies to you.

Married at 18, Divorced at 30

*M*y Memaw once told me, "A woman that is looking for a husband has never had one." LOL Let's face it, we can't help but to keep our eyes peeled for that one guy we have been dreaming of, ever since we witnessed Cinderella fall in love with the Prince, or watched Belle dance with the Beast.

"Excuse me, virgin girl, I found my man of God - preaching machine when I was 18 years old! I was married at 19 and have two beautiful babies!" To you, Mrs. Whoever.... I say congratulations. My mother married at 17, and today, my parents have been married for 35 years. I'm not talking to the ladies who have found the man God had for them. Many of my friends have found their soulmate early in life, however, this book is not for them. This book is for all of us single women who are sexy, saved, and waiting for a Godly man that we are actually attracted to. *(fingers crossed)*

Right now, I want to talk to the girls that feel their only way out of their bad situations is to get married. I'm talking to the girl whose only dream is to have dinner ready by five-thirty for her husband, who is actually playing around with his secretary. **Yes, you!** The girl who wants nothing more in life, then to feel loved by a man, because she's never experienced the love of God. Put down the proverbial spatula! It's time to start serving GOD!

Maybe you were the girl so in love with a man, you didn't see anything else in life. He was your all and all - the butter to your bread. Listen little lady, he's gonna look a lot different 20 years from now. I'm just saying, there may or may not be a beer belly in your future family photos. What I just said may have offended someone, and I don't apologize for that. *Get back on track Vic…*

I'm sick of seeing young women so in love with the idea of marriage and popping babies out, that they will settle for anything or anyone to make it a reality. They have no idea what marriage and motherhood are all about, and more importantly, what God says they are about. They are not yet aware of who they are as women. They leave no room for God to have any say in the future plans of their lives, because they are fooled by the thought of having someone to love, will solve all of their problems. That's where it gets tricky, finding the right one to love you. Just because you found a man, doesn't mean he's *THE MAN*.

If you are filled with the love and voice of God, He will make sure the right one is loving you.

So, let's stop trying to make something happen with someone, that's not supposed to happen. It will happen in His perfect timing. Let God fill you up and grow you up!

Marriage is not the answer, if you are empty. Marriage is ONLY the answer if you are FULL. You cannot give when you are empty. God did not create Adam a wife until Adam, himself, was FULLY CREATED. It wasn't until He was finished creating Adam, that God put him to sleep and TOOK from him to create his wife, Eve.

Get this: let God build you, mold you, *(mess you up, per say)* and when he is finished, He will put you to sleep. In other words, you'll be CHILLIN' OUT - Relaxin' - Maxin' all Cool - knowing God is creating for you the most perfect masterpiece... YOUR soul mate. *DING!* When you least expect it, *BAM*, there he/she will be.

Now the Lord God said, "It is not good for man to be alone. I will make a helper suitable for him. Now the Lord God had formed out of the ground all the wild animals and all the birds in the sky. He brought them to the man to see what he would name them; and whatever the man called each living creature, that was its name. So the man gave names to all the livestock, the birds in the sky and all the wild animals. But for Adam no suitable helper was found. So the Lord God caused the man to fall into a deep sleep; and while he was sleeping, he took one of the man's ribs and then closed up the place with flesh. Then the Lord God made a woman from the rib he had taken out of the man, and he brought her to the man. The man said, "This is now bone of my bones and flesh of my flesh; she shall be called 'woman,' for she was taken out of man. Genesis 2:18-24 Sidenote! It's cool that God was letting Adam pick who he found suitable for himself. He's like, "Oohhhh no, God! None of these animals will do!" Ha! God wants you to really enjoy your mate. Don't put so much pressure on yourself. God wants you to have the desires of your heart.

Let's *REWIND!* As I said before, Adam had to be complete before God brought Eve to him. *If he wasn't complete, God wouldn't have had the right ingredients to take from Adam and create Eve.* If He tried to make her before all the ingredients were there, she would have been a half-baked hot mess. Adam didn't even realize he was alone before Eve came along, so he was content with his purpose - the task of naming the animals and exploring the Earth. We have to be content with the call of God on our lives, and we can't allow the gifts God has given us to lay dormant. We need to be busy working in the abilities He has given us, so that the person He brings to us, will fit perfectly into the will of God for our lives.

I believe that God's timing is perfect whether you are 18 when you find your soulmate, or whether you are 45. What may seem to us like an eternity of singleness, is only a blink of an eye for Him. It amazes me how much God cares about our lives and how thorough He is at orchestrating them. His timing is perfect and He will never bring anything or anyone to us that we are not ready for. There should never be a *"rush"* when it comes to marriage. It's not a race. I don't understand why so many of my peers are dying to get married. They are literally obsessed with it. *JUST CHILL OUT!* You have the rest of your life to be married! If you're so desperately confused as to why you haven't come in contact with your significant other, it is because our God is a good daddy, and He will not bring you something *YOU ARE NOT READY FOR!* If all you do is crave someone else's attention, you are not capable of giving any away. You will just be a little love leach. Nobody wants a desperate love-sucker, sucking every ounce of energy out of them. *That's unattractive.*

TRUST ME! I WANT TO GET MARRIED. However, I feel, overall, our generation of women are consumed and overwhelmed with men and trying to attain one. I feel as though we believe this is where our purpose and our security will come from. Some of us have no real purpose of our own. This fosters our identities to be placed in the guy we are currently dating. We may think we are getting closer to the perfect marriage by chasing all of these men, but in reality we are driving ourselves further away from it. We are preventing the right person from entering our lives. We are wasting precious time, time that God created for us to grow into the women we were purposed to be.

Redeem the time because the days are evil. Ephesians 5:16

It's not Godly to waste your time. So all the time and energy you are spending on the wrong person, is actually ungodly. You're not just playing around, missy, you're affecting your future - your destiny. You were given a certain amount of time on this Earth to accomplish certain tasks. Falling in love over and over and tying yourself to losers, is not something God intended for you to do. He didn't envision you being divorced before you get a car insurance break at 25. *You have to be wise with your time!* You only have one life to live. Calm down and trust God to bring you the right person. Work on your future, your talents, your God given abilities, then the big fish will start swimming in your pond. Those are the kind of fish that will become marriage material ladies.

Jane Doe thinks that John Doe will complete her life when they find one another. You can't go into a marriage needing to be fixed when you're already broken. Only when you are complete in yourself, and your partner is complete in themselves, can God join you together.

I want to pause and tell you about a young friend of mine named **Tosha.** I have never seen anyone like her. She can fall in love with almost anyone. I love her dearly and don't want this story in any way to look like I'm judging her or disrespecting her. We all go through things. We all make mistakes. Everybody has one of those days. I want to tell her story, because I think it will help someone.

TOSHA

...The Desperate Lover

Tosha was in and out of an abusive relationship throughout her high school career. I remember hearing a story once, where he took a bat to her windshield and even dislocated her arm. I'm telling you, it was rough, especially for a young 16-year-old girl to go through. I can't even imagine going through something like this. He would beat her. He would call her names. She kept going back to him over and over again and for some strange reason, she thought he was going to change every single time. We all thought she was crazy. We would hear about horrible incidents, then see them walking hand in hand at church that very Sunday! She eventually became pregnant by this guy at age 18, then they were engaged. He continued to beat her and lash out in anger towards her. So she breaks up with him just to get back together later on. This cycle goes on and on. Luckily, Tosha was finally able to break free from the abusive relationship after years of this horrible abuse.

Next, she turned to dating apps and hooking up. She found a winner, at last, and married him. She packed everything up and moved herself and her son across the country for a man she barely knew. It wasn't long before she discovered he wasn't a very good guy, and they filed for divorce. With embarrassment and shame, she moved herself and her son back in with her mother. The divorce wasn't final before she met another fantastic man on her faithful dating app. After a few weeks, he became husband #2. *(of course he did)* But to her surprise, that ended abruptly.

I don't know exactly what forms this kind of need for affection, all I know is that it is not of God. Her son has had to see 5 or 6 men come in and out of his life. It breaks my heart. By the age of 21, she has had a child, been engaged three times, and divorced twice.

This is one of thousands of stories of young women who are forced to carry more baggage than a bellhop, before they are even old enough to rent a car. This may be your story. You may be like Tosha, searching for love and fulfillment in all the wrong places. Trapped time and time again in relationships that are suffocating you, drowning you, leaving you without true love. It's time to let God's love fill you. It's time to redirect your path, and get your mind right about the idea of marriage.

Another spin on the Merry-Go-Round

*D*ifferent guy, same crap, on this man filled merry-go-round.
When you drop the wrong people from your life, the right things start to happen.

Bad relationships are in some sense like Merry-Go-Rounds. So many different stallions to choose from. After getting rid of the first one, we see one that's a bit shinier than the last one. We say, *"Oh that one will be fun!"* Only to find out it's going in the same direction as the other. No matter how many times you change your mind and switch to another stallion, you keep going around and around getting nowhere. After trying out 10 different animals, you will find yourself spinning around in circles on the little bench in the midst of the beautiful stallions all alone. No ring on your finger, no healthy relationship, not even a consistent date night. You're once again broken-hearted and having to pick up the pieces of a broken relationship that didn't work out for you.

You may be falling for the same type over and over again because of your personality type and/or spiritual gifts.

If God created you with the gift to lead and to go against the grain, you may be allowing yourself to slip into a lifestyle of rebellion with the bad boy. The enemy will try and pervert your God given abilities and gifts, and use them against you. Make sure your gifts are your strength, and not your weakness. If you are a compassionate, forgiving person, be careful not to let people run over you. If you, by nature, love change and adventure, make sure you aren't giving your body away to men who don't deserve it. Your gift can be your struggle, but that is why we have the Holy Spirit to help guide and lead us into all truth.

But when he, the Spirit of truth, comes, he will guide you into all truth. John 16:13

The word of God will always be honest and true and keep you on course. If you are ever worried that you are not using your God given abilities to further His kingdom, pick up the Bible and read it!

It amazes me how we keep falling for men that have the same character traits and habits that we say we can't stand. Most of the time we say we want a certain type of man and end up gravitating towards the complete opposite. *Why do we do that?* Why do we settle for less than what we want, better yet, less than what we deserve! Why eat spam from the can, when the steak has been marinated and ready to grill? We've put so much time into preparing the table to look special for a big meal. We googled the best ways to marinate the steak and after all that preparation, we get frustrated because the steak is taking too long to cook. Why are we so ignorant! If we could just discipline ourselves enough to wait the extra time, we could be enjoying a great meal. We are too impatient, and can't chill long enough for the steak to finish. So we end up grabbing the spam from the cabinet and satisfying our hunger with something that won't properly nourish our bodies. We do this in relationships often. We know in our hearts that God is preparing a wonderful man for us. We pray for him, we ask God to prepare us for him, and we ask that he would find us - but we end up dating the schmucks with no future and 3 kids on the way by 3 different women. Then God has to smack us upside the head and our hearts become broken yet again. More soul ties are formed with a person that was never even meant to kiss our lips!

I have been a testimony to this kind of horrific behavior as have many of my single friends *(excluding Miss Walters, my only virgin friend, she is the strongest woman known to mankind)*. Actually, let me tell you a little bit about Andrea, Miss Walters, the Saint of all Saints. ;)

ANDREA

...The Saint

Words from the phenomenon, herself. *"I'm 29 years old... Wow. There have been seasons that have been easier than others. I feel that God revealed this one consistent thought to me in my anxiousness to get married and fight to stay pure. He said to me, "Andrea, look at me, I am content. I'm not impatient or anxious about my bride, my bride being you. I'm waiting on you."* As HE is, so am I in the world. *He is on the throne, chillin'. I don't have to stress, He's not stressed. He knows who I'm going to be with... and if He can wait on me, I can wait on the one He is sending to me. There have been men I thought were "it", but in the end, if it wasn't God's will I gave it back to Jesus. God's got it."*

Andrea is a virgin and absolutely full of the joy of God. She is one of the most confident women I have ever known, and she's never even allowed her lips to touch a man's lips. Her willingness to wait is astonishing to me. It's obvious to me that her relationship and love for Jesus keeps her full of joy and laughter. She remains unmarked by sexual immorality and is such an inspiration to me. I love you, dear friend.

I wish I could say that my life has been a lot like Andrea's, but to be honest, it hasn't. Yes, we are both virgins, but my strength has failed me many times. I've bailed on my promises to God as I have indulged in the wrong relationships. So many times I have said I wanted a good guy who loves God with all his heart. A man who would treat me with respect...but I would end up with a bad boy that conflicted with my character. A man who may come to church once in a blue moon, just because I nagged about it. Or maybe for you, you fell for the jealous guy or the clinger - or my personal favorite, the guy who shows interest in you once every couple weeks then disappears. Gets me every time.

REBECCA

...The Abused Angel

My beautiful Rebecca may be the most incredible woman on the planet, besides my mother of course. This is a woman I've known since I was 9 months old and I consider her nothing less than a sister. When she walks into a room everyone instantly feels love, as she leads with grace every word that comes out of her mouth. Her class is incomparable. Her beauty is unmatched. Rebecca was always special. By the age of 8 yrs old, she had a visitation from Heaven and spoke in tongues for 3 days straight *(If you do not believe in tongues...you should... sorry, not sorry)*. From that time on, she saw things in the spirit like no other child I have ever seen, known, or even heard about. Seeing Angels was completely normal to her. I remember her saying to her sister and I, *"Gals, do you see those Angels dancing over there?!"* Of course we never saw anything. We would just stare in awe as she gazed into the spirit world. Beth and I always had little boyfriends here and there during high school, but Rebecca was different. She was very cautious to never date or attach herself to anyone, and she seemed totally content with it. I would often wish I could be more like her in that area. It was not until she was 21 years old that she had a serious boyfriend. They met on Facebook and then agreed to meet in the nearest city for coffee. At first she told us he was too short and totally not her type! He grossed her out! How is it that these gross dudes creep in like lions on the prowl, turning our pure thoughts into filthy ones. Rebecca was not the same woman after just a few months with this dude. He considered himself a *"man of God"* yet he began to control her in ways she had never been controlled before. He began to tell her what she could and couldn't do, like he was her spiritual advisor or something. For example: She wasn't allowed to wear red lipstick in public, because he was afraid other men would find her attractive. She was not allowed to watch the movie Twilight, because he considered it ungodly *(Maybe it is, but that wasn't his place to decide for her)*. Her confidence was being torn apart day after day. She wasn't allowed to accept male friend requests on Facebook and God forbid if she shook the hand of the opposite sex. Insanity is what this relationship was and there was no getting through to her.

__Her eyes were fixed on him like a moth to a flame; it was only a matter of time before she got burnt.__

If you are trapped in a controlling relationship and you don't know how to get away, surround yourself with people who can pull you out. Take back control of your life. Don't let the enemy of your soul steal one more day of your purity and sanity! *YOU ARE WORTH MORE!* You don't have to be controlled by his sweet talk or gestures of sexual pleasure. **YOU ARE A WOMAN** of fierce beauty, don't let anyone control you or tell you how you should live your life, unless they are Jesus himself. I told you it was only a matter of time before she got burned, and that is exactly what happened. This jealous freak ended up cheating on her with a friend of hers! Wow, ladies... doesn't that just tick you off! I'm freaking ticked off right now just writing about it! This guy who controlled her every move, was actually the one cheating on her! What a hypocrite!

The jealous type is a scary type to get involved with. There is a reason why they are jealous. A lot of the time they are doing the very thing they are afraid you might be doing, and that provokes them to be jealous and overprotective.

Recognize what type of guy you keep falling for. For me personally, I feel as if I had seasons where I fell for the same type of guy. As for others you might be falling for the same type of guy your entire life. When I was young, I would go through stages where I would only be attracted to a certain type of boy. It's actually really weird when I think about it. I guess the answer is: As I would grow, then my taste for boys would grow. Just like my style of clothing or music at the time. Sometimes I would grow in the wrong direction, and sometimes in the right one. However, I have to say, no matter how many boys I would try to make it work with, I always go back to wanting a guy who loved God the way that I did. Those kind of men may be harder to find but, nevertheless, with patience we must keep our focus on that type - the perfect type - the type that we know deep down in our hearts is the kind of guy our Jesus would want for us.

Why do we settle for the guy that doesn't fit our standards?! Why do we, as women, allow our lives to keep going around and around - until one day we are alone in our bedrooms sleeping next to this guy that was never what we wanted! This wasn't the guy we asked God for when we were 12 years old. The man we dreamt about. The man we prayed for. We find ourselves stuck.

The kind of guy you keep falling for says a lot about your character, and what you lack in your own personal life. I have a friend that didn't have a father figure growing up, so she only dates older men who tend to treat her like a daughter; which isn't necessarily a bad thing. We need to recognize why we keep attracting the same type of guy, and if in fact there is something wrong with us. We need to allow God to reveal to us what needs to change.

I have another friend that always falls for the control freak type of guys. They always have to know where she's at every second of every day. She could never have fun with her girlfriends, and if we ever do go out, he's always accusing her of cheating on him. It makes me sick! You have to figure out why you keep falling for these same types of sick, nasty guys. When you recognize the type, then you can examine your own self and say; *"Hey now, girl! Why are you falling for these dudes every time?"* Let's go through a few types of guys and the warning signs:

TYPES:

Calvin the Clinger

Red flags: If he wants to tag along on girl's night, his name may be Calvin. There's a reason why it's called

GIRL's Night. If he's obsessing over unresponsive texts, his name is Calvin. Calvin is probably very insecure, so take note.

Walter the Whiner

Red Flags: If he's whining about not being able to hold your hand long enough, *(even though you are both hiking up a mountain and sweating profusely)* he may be a Whiny Walter. *"Do you not like meeeeeeee, hold my hand, pleaseeeeee, it makes me feel like you don't like meeeeee! My other girlfriends couldn't keep their hands off me! Victoriaaaaaaaa"* Omg! This is Walter the Whiner!

Chris The Control Freak

Red Flags: He insists that you keep your *"read receipts"* and *"shared location"* on at all times. He asks mutual friends where you are every time you walk out of the house. Wants to be near you to make sure you are behaving the way he wants you to, and that you act and look the way he wants you to as well! Chris needs to be kicked to the curb!

John the Jealous Gigolo

Red Flags: John is a cheater. John assumes, because he is cheating you must be cheating too. Therefore, he is jealous of every single interaction that takes place between you and another male. He is simply projecting his behavior on to you. Buh-Byeee, JOHN!

Abusive Adrian

Red Flag: In most cases, Adrian exhibits most of the above behavior, plus he'll probably beat the crap out of you, emotionally or physically. Adrian deserves to be put in jail. CALL THE POLICE!

Seth the Sex Addict

Red Flag: If he is repulsed by the thought of waiting to have sex and is cheating on you because you want to wait…. he's probably a sex addict. If the only dates he takes you on are to his bedroom, he only cares about sex. If he only contacts you late at night, he just wants SEX! If he keeps pushing the sexual limits further and further, he doesn't care about your morals or desires to remain pure. He just wants SEX! Seth deserves a slap.

Billy the Bum

Red Flag: If you are on your first date, and he *"forgets his wallet"*, it may have been an accident. However, if by the second and third time you are out with him, and he still can't seem to keep track of "his wallet", he's a BUM! *Get a J.O.B.*

I'm not saying that any man is perfect. None of us are perfect. We all have flaws, but some of us aren't working towards bettering ourselves, and that is the kind of guy you do not want to be with. If he doesn't recognize what he's doing to you, and is pushing you in a negative direction, you need to dump him. Most importantly, if he doesn't care about becoming the man he needs to be for you, then you need to ditch him.

I know as women most of the time we feel as if we can fix any and every man. Transforming them into who they need to be for us and for God. Only God can change a person's soul. We are most definitely called to show them love and hope, but we don't have to sleep with them to do so. That almost never works.

You don't have a magic holy vagina. Jesus is not an STD, and try as you may, you cannot sexually transmit Him to your man. Having sex with the person you are trying to fix, doesn't fix anything. You will probably forget what you were trying to fix in the first place, because you run the risk of being *"blinded by love."* Love truly is blind and that can be scary. Without our eyes we can walk straight into all kinds of danger. If we are without our feelers, there is no way to detect danger or harm.

BETH

...The Blind Lover

Beth… how do I even describe her? You simply just have to meet her, friends! But… I'll give it a try. She's tall. She has short black hair, big lips, hips, and fingertips. She's stunning. She's full of life and enthusiasm. She's absolutely off the wall crazy, but at the same time, she is very reserved. She's been my best friend ever since we realized we were wearing the same shirt one Sunday. I can't exactly remember, but I do believe we were around the age of 4. Although, we actually spent most days by one another's side before that eye opening Sunday. The shirt situation just took our friendship to a whole new level. We did everything together: double dates, touring the country with our Christian Rock band, heading to the suburbs of Chicago for Bible College, and as children; torturing old folk every Sunday by passing around pre-licked cookies from the nursery. For most of our lives, we have never been without one another....that was until John came along.

Beth met John when she was 15 years old, and of course I was with her at the time. She was waitressing at a restaurant in our hometown when he came in on his lunch break. He flirted with her and quickly got her phone number. She didn't know it at the time, but he was actually 9 years older than she was. They began to talk and he offered her an even better waitressing job at his family's restaurant. Soooo...optimistic Beth took him up on that offer.

They agreed to meet up and head over to the restaurant where she would have her first interview. I was with her of course, along with her older sister Rebecca *(another friend I speak of in this book),* who rounds out our little trilogy. All four of us crammed into his beaten up truck, and got on our way. Everything was normal at first, then police lights lit up behind us. We were completely freaking out, because we were four deep in this three passenger truck. The police officer came to the car as we were holding our breath. He asks John to get out and follow him. John was gone for quite a few minutes, before we finally got the nerve to turn around. I may have been the first to peek. *"Guys, the cop is doing a freaking breathalyzer test on him!"* The girls quickly turned their heads around... We sat silent. Our eyes glued to the current situation in front of us. We were terrified. The three of us are indisputably the definition of *Good Girls*... especially at this age. We had never witnessed anyone being administered a breathalyzer test. Oh, and by the way it was only noon! The police officer then began to cuff him and take him away. We were left completely alone on the side of the road with a stranger's truck. Apparently, he had a warrant out for his arrest and was also intoxicated! Of course, we did not call our parents. Instead, we called a friend of ours who was much older, and not so much of a *Good Girl* as we were. We knew she wouldn't judge our ignorant ways. *(Always call your parents. We were idiots)*

This was the beginning of Beth and John, a relationship that would almost ruin my beloved friend. It didn't start off bad, it never does. However, I feel the need to fast forward ten years after the car incident. Yes, ten years. The only time Beth was free from him was when we were away at Bible College for two years. As soon as we returned back home, she returned to him.

John wasn't all-bad in the beginning. He was a very giving person, who wanted great things in life. As time went on he began to turn his focus toward the wrong vices. Drugs began to consume him. Turning him into a con artist. He sold whatever he could get his hands on in order to obtain drugs. He became whomever he had to become to stay out of jail, and stay in Beth's good graces. He was emotionally abusive, a thief, and a liar. He was a master manipulator. He preyed on Beth's weaknesses, and kept her bound in fear and eventually debt.

Everything was revealed when I received a disturbing phone call, *(from the same friend that picked us up from the side of the road that day when we first met John thank GOD for you, Tracy. You have always come to our rescue)* while I was living in Minneapolis, and Beth in Nashville. My friend began to tell me that John had posted a disturbing video of Beth online, and that hundreds of people had already seen it! She sent it to me and I couldn't speak. I was horrified. He was screaming like a maniac, cursing, and pushing her. Her face was buried in her lap and she wasn't saying a word most of the time. She was like a zombie without any expression or emotion. Throughout this video, he continued to follow her around and terrorize her. She had to use the restroom and He wouldn't allow her to do so. I'll just let your imagination tell the rest of the story. I'll never know why he posted such a horrible video of himself to HER social media account, because he looked like an absolute idiot! I am however, very thankful he did because it was enough to get her away from him. My friend that called me about the video rescued Beth that very night.

Even though Beth is now in terrible financial debt, and she is still uncovering more items John stole from her and then sold for drug money; she is free! She's herself again. She's filled with confidence again. In a matter of weeks, God has restored her. Yes, she will have to pay for the mistakes she has made, mostly financially, but she is still FREE! The scars of this long relationship will always be there, but SHE GOT AWAY, and God will do the rest. He will repair her.

It's never going to be as hard as you think it is! No matter what the situation is, *YOU CAN GET OUT!* Money can't hold you. Insecurities can't hold you. Abuse can't hold you. When God says it's done, it's done, and no one can do anything about it. The most amazing part of this story is, God knew the very day she would become free of him. She just had to comply. She had to choose to say yes. I'm sure God gave Beth many chances to escape prior to this day. In fact, I know without a doubt He did. However, that exact day God had about all He could take. Enough was enough. It always amazes me to watch God do His thing. We would have talk after talk with Beth regarding this guy. We did all we could do to try and get her away, but God was in complete control. He's so very faithful to take care of us while we are acting like crazy fools, then wash us off when we come home. He not only washes us off but, He celebrates our homecoming as well. It's as if we never made one mistake. The devil will cripple you in fear to keep you in horrible situations. Don't listen to his lies. Run to the arms of Jesus and don't look back!

"When he came to his senses, he said, 'How many of my father's hired servants have food to spare, and here I am starving to death! I will set out and go back to my father and say to him: Father I have sinned against heaven and against you. I am no longer worthy to

113

be called your son; make me like one of your hired servants.' So he got up and went to his father. But while he was still a long way off, his father saw him and was filled with compassion for him; he ran to his son, and threw his arms around him and kissed him. The son said to him, 'Father, I have sinned against heaven and against you. I am no longer worthy to be called your son.' But the father said to the servants, 'Quick! Bring the best robe and put it on him. Put a ring on his finger and sandals on his feet. Bring the fattened calf and kill it. Let's have a feast and celebrate. For this son of mine was dead and is alive again; he was lost and is found.' So they began to celebrate." Luke 15:17-24

DO NOT STAY IN A RELATIONSHIP THAT IS SUFFOCATING YOUR DREAM, YOUR MONEY, and most importantly YOUR RELATIONSHIP WITH God.

God will restore everything back to Beth, because His love never ends. It's everlasting. She's no longer drowning, and all the glory goes to God.

So don't be afraid; you are worth more than many sparrows. Matt 10:31

For God has not given us a spirit of fear and timidity, but of power, love, and self-discipline. 2 Timothy 1:7 NLT

This is my command — be strong and courageous! Do not be afraid or discouraged. For the Lord your God is with you wherever you go.

Joshua 1:9

What kind of guy do you NEED to fall for? A man after God's heart, is a man for whom your heart deserves. A man who has dreams that align with yours is a man who deserves a second look. A man who will lead you in the right direction, is a man you should envision fathering your children. It's time that we begin to allow these things to sink in. The *man-filled Merry-Go-Round* will always let us down. It will leave us dizzy and confused. We have to step off this ride and believe again! Trust again that God will do what He told our hearts he would do. I know in my heart God will bring me the man that I truly need, the man that will fulfill my dreams; because I have stepped off this crazy ride. **Wait on the man that compliments your life in such a way that everything goes to the next level.**

Maybe you're saying, *"I can't help it that I'm only attracted to guys that do me wrong!"* Girrrrl! You better change what you're attracted to, before you end up lost and broken! I do believe that you have to be attracted to someone to marry them, don't hear me wrong. That is why God gave us emotions, feelings, hormones, and everything that makes a female a female. But, we have to decide what we want to be attracted to in a man and stick to those guidelines and desires.

I once found myself in a *"set up"* situation. A minister I know set me up with this really great guy. He had everything going for him, but I was not in any way attracted to him. They pushed me very hard to ignore those feelings and promised me that love would come. I was TERRIFIED! Probably the most stressed out I had ever been. I thought I was going to have to marry someone I did not like, and that was just sickening to me. I tried to think about kissing him and I wanted to vomit... So how was this guy supposed to be my soul mate?! I believe 100% that with God's guidance you will know, maybe not in the first 5 minutes, but eventually you will know. You will know without a doubt that he is the one you need to be with and be very attracted to him. As Christian women we don't have to settle! We should never settle.

The tricky part is, our flesh can be extremely attracted to someone that is entirely wrong for us, and we can even fall in love with them. In my experience it has been very easy for me to fall for guys that are not right for me. It's called *lust* ladies and your stinking flesh, they will both cause you to ignore advice, reality, and sometimes even God; in hopes to keep that man your body has to have. **Just because the candy tastes good, doesn't mean we can eat endless amounts of its sweet goodness!** Candy won't suffice for breakfast, lunch, and dinner. Just because he feels and looks good, doesn't mean he is good.

"Everything is permissible for me, but not everything is beneficial. 'Everything is permissible for me' – but I will not be mastered by anything." I Corinthians 6:12

The Bible says that He will give us the desires of our heart. I believe if we can manage to stop falling for the same lame guys, and just be patient our perfect package will arrive right on time. God wants to give us the man of our dreams and it is our job to be patient and ready for him.

I'm not saying the man or the situation in which you meet him will be perfect, but I believe it will be in His will, and that is exactly where you want to be. This is where we find true happiness and contentment. Knowing that God approves of our lives is the most liberating feeling there is. Maybe this is why we feel anxious, angry, annoyed, on edge, or on the defense, regarding our men when people say we are with the wrong person. This is because we hear, *"You're out of the will of God,"* and deep down inside we know it. We know he is not God's number one pick for us.

Oh, dear girls. We've gotta let God have control and trust that He knows what He's doing, or we will be married at 20 and divorced by 40; simply because we didn't believe God could bring us the guy we've dreamt about since we were little girls. Quit lying to yourself. If he does not live up to God's standards **LET GO** and **LET God** have control. And here's something else: Do you believe God is good? Ok, then just chill out and let Him be GOOD to you!

Chicken Balls

He flew me to Paris...

If someone were to come up to you and say, *"In one month, a cute boy will fly you to his city from across the country, in his father's plane; just to meet you for a few hours..."* Would you believe them? What if they also said, *"He also owns a small mansion in a wealthy neighborhood, just beneath one of the most spectacular mountain ranges this side of the Mississippi. He works in his parents' megachurch and will one day take over as lead pastor. He's been watching you sing on television for 6 months (where was I on television?). He will fly you to Paris and back, (because he will learn later it has been your dream since you were a little girl to see the romantic city with your own eyes) just to give you a rose at a floral shop across the street from the Eiffel Tower."* Would you pee your freaking panties or what? Well, it happened to me, and it was the most difficult heart I've ever had to break...

To my beloved aunts and grandmother, he was perfect. Let me start from the very beginning. It was a frigid morning in Munster, IN, and I never dreamed that this day would hold so much promise. The double bed at the Gallego's household we both slept in wasn't so large due to Beth's long legs, and her tendency to stretch them out while sleeping. We lived with a wonderful *Latin* family and two pit bulls in the south suburbs of Chicago, where we both felt safe and loved. It was far different from our small town life in Kentucky, and we enjoyed every second of it.

The alarms on both mine and Beth's iPhones blared underneath our pillows, as we both let out terrifying moans of pain; *(suddenly aware of our lack of sleep)*, due to us acting like insane people, just hours before. We never looked good on Mondays, and we were ok with that. The church we were involved in had 5 services on the weekend, and we were heavily involved in all of them, whether that meant leading praise and worship or volunteering in the children's departments. Sunday night was the only evening we were free to have fun, so every Sunday *(after our church services)*, we headed downtown to hang out with our new friends we made in the city.

I'm not sure why we never thought of class the next morning.

When Monday came around, we were both super zonked. It was 9:50am and we had just enough time to get our old sweats on, brush our teeth, put our hair in a bun; and get to class by 10am. We never ate breakfast, because sleep was so much better. We ran downstairs in our shoes *(our Mexi Papa would have killed us, if he knew our shoes touched his clean carpet)*, grabbed bottled waters, and kissed *Baby* and *Bella* before heading out the garage door. The car ride to class never consisted of more than a few words, most of the time it was, *"Uhhhhhhh"* or *"Ohhhhh God..."*

Our classes were long and brutal, but on this particular Monday, (although sleepy and hungry) we were excited about an Indian Professor, who was in town to instruct our class. He was a man we loved and respected very much. He knew his stuff and could hold our attention no matter how long the sessions were. He had over 1,500 churches in India, and I would often dream of the day that I could afford to go to one of them and sing.

At 9:59 AM we walked into the small classroom where only a handful of other students were seated. Beth and I were the only two Caucasian students, which I personally loved. Lots of laughter and soul in that little room... that's the way I liked it. One classmate in particular sticks out in my mind. I don't recall her name, all I remember are her wide hips and bustin' boobs she would flaunt to class everyday. I especially loved when she would *"feel the spirit"* and scream out, *"YESSSSUUUUUHHHH! YESSSSUHHHHH!"*, and clap extremely fast while stomping on the floor. If you haven't figured it out already, I attended Bible College at a predominately black school. A school full of some of the most incredible people I have ever met. People who would become my friends and soon after my family. I had never felt so at home in all my life.

We were greeted by our favorite Indian Professor as we walked in, *"Ohhhh VictoDia and Bed, so good do see you."* We loved him and his wife so very much. This class would be the very last class we had with them before graduating. We were trying our best to stay awake and soak it all in. This is where it gets interesting. To conclude our time with him he suggested a few moments of prayer. He asked everyone to bring a wallet, car keys, or anything that would represent prosperity in our lives to the front. I calmly and discreetly slipped my *"true love waits"* ring into the palm of my hand, wanting prayer for my future husband. There is no way he could have seen me do this. I did it very stealth-like, and I told no one. Beth grabbed her car keys, and we walked up front. She, believing for a new car, and I, wanting prayer for the man that would one day call me his wife.

He prayed for others in line ahead of me and then suddenly, as if lightning flashed where I stood, he looked at me and said, *"I have a man you need to meet. I believe he is the one for you."* My heart started to race with excitement. The butterflies in my stomach began to float, making a gentle escape upwards, soaring all the way to my brain - invading my thoughts and imagination. I was sure they had permeated my skull in a way that left them hovering above me, hanging there for everyone to see.

"There was no way he could have seen my ring in my hand", I thought to myself. *"THIS HAD TO HAVE BEEN GOD!"* after all, how could it not have been? My emotions went crazy. I could not wait to meet this man I knew nothing about.

The class ended, we said our goodbyes to the professor and his precious wife, and then we headed to the car. Beth and I began to scream and jump while holding hands in the parking lot... *(as only two girls excited about the prospect of a new love do)* We both believed I was about to meet my future husband!

"Can you believe he just said that to you?!", Beth said. We giggled and talked about the future with excitement in our voices, as we drove home for a long nap. Months went by and I almost forgot my Professor ever said anything to me about this perfect man for me. All excitement was gone, and I honestly thought he had just forgotten, until one day my phone began to ring in my back pocket. I remember I was upstairs overlooking the gym at the church I worked in at that time. I looked down and saw that it was an international number, and for some reason I picked up.

"VictoDia! How do you do today?" I knew by the strong Indian accent, it was my professor. He began to tell me about this preacher's son that I was going to meet very soon, and how much he thought I would like him. He then gave me HIS NAME! Dun dun dun... *(Cue horror music soundtrack)* I rushed over to my best friend, *(Andrea. She and I developed this friendship while I was away at Bible College)* and gave her the name of the mystery man! Andrea is quite the character, and she has insanely awesome stalker skills. We began to search for him on every social media network possible! *AND WE COULDN'T FIND ANYTHING!* Eventually, we found his parents' church website and were very impressed. It appeared to be a very large church, which made me super giddy. She and I both agreed this had to be the one for me. I know Jesus was laughing at us, because He knew once I laid eyes on this boy, I would be completely turned off. Why He allowed me to go through such an adventure, I will never know, but I'm glad he did. For now, I can tell you

about it, and all I learned from it. The Bible says that He is a mysterious God, and I'm so glad that He is. He makes my life absolutely marvelous and intriguing.

A few months went by from the time I received the phone call from the professor, and the day I would meet this mystery guy. I still hadn't communicated with this mystery man, Billy. *(the guy I researched with Andrea)* I had been communicating with my professor and he continued to tell me over and over, that he believed God had spoken to him that this was the man for me. Billy believed this as well. I really had this thing built up in my head. I was so nervous and excited. My little brother was in town on the day I was supposed to meet this guy *and HIS DAD.* Thank God I didn't have to go through this alone. Complete strangers were flying on their private jet to come meet simple ole' me for just a few hours! *THAT'S A LOT OF PRESSURE PEOPLE!* I got myself all beautified that morning and thought to myself, *"Today is the day you will meet your husband."* I couldn't believe he was coming all this way just to meet me. This was surreal. This was my own personal fairytale. Wow… this was the day. My brother and I got in the Jag and took off…here we go! By the way, my friend Andrea threatened to hide in the restaurant at her own table, to watch it all go down. That was until I threatened her life. What was funny is, I had to stop and get some gas before heading to the restaurant, and I ran into the guy I was sort of dating at the time. He asked me where I was going. I was so thrilled I had the opportunity to rub what was about to happen in his face. For the last 2 years he had been leading me on and not making our relationship official *(Girls, do we hate that, or what? Beyonce once said, "If you like it, put a ring on it!")*. I was like, *"Take that, you little stinker, you lost your freakin' chance, BOOM!"* That shows you how much of a sense of humor God has. He allowed me to run into my crush on the way to meet the guy I thought was going to be THE ONE! I drove off looking hot as ever about to meet the man of my dreams. I remember turning around towards the door as he walked in... There he was with my professor and his father. Gulp... He didn't look too bad, except for the fact I could tell he would be bald by the age of 35. *(please don't be offended... just letting you in on my most personal thoughts.)* His style of dress was great though. He was probably super cute to most girls. Unfortunately, unlike most girls, I'm extremely hard to please. Which is probably why I'm still single. He had beautiful blue eyes, a nice muscular build, styled light brown hair *(that hair gel...ew)*, and a strong handshake, like really really awkwardly stong. He sat at the table, and I talked my head off. I honestly wasn't attracted to him. *(this is something I do when I don't like someone)*.. I pushed those feelings aside and tried to accept the fact that this was probably the man for me. I mean everything else seemed to add up, so how could he not be? He was perfect in all sorts of ways: he loved God, worked in the church, had *LOTS* of money, and he really liked me. I know now that God was teaching me all sorts of things while going through this. I should've stood up for myself from the very beginning and let everyone know what I was feeling in my heart. I didn't feel anything for this stranger, not even the slightest spark. I was being pressured into becoming this guy's woman, and I didn't say a word about it. I was trying to please everyone around me, and it was about to get me into a lot of trouble; and a lot of wasted time. I was also about to hurt someone very badly who never deserved to be hurt in the first place.

God gives us emotions for a reason. I believe He wants you to be absolutely in love with the person He has for you. *DO NOT* settle until you fall head over heels. God wants it to be that way. He wants you to have the love and the goods. He wants to give you the good guy, and the guy you are madly in love with - all at the same time. Don't ever settle because someone tells you that you need to, or make you think that this is the best you can ever hope to get! Girl, if you aren't completely feeling a dude, do not be afraid to let him go just because you don't want to be alone! Wait on the one God truly has for you, no matter how long it takes.

Everyone around me seemed to think that this guy was so perfect for me. I don't like to be wrong, and I struggle with the fear of being unsuccessful, and this guy seemed to have it all together. I decided to engage in a relationship with him, because it seemed comfortable. He flew me to his state across the country countless times, and even had a room built for me in his parents' mansion. Let me tell you this, I was treated like a princess by these wonderful people, and I was - and still am - so appreciative of all they did for me. This made it that much harder to let everyone know, I was in complete misery the entire time. I would cry myself to sleep, scared to death I would have to marry this man that I didn't love. I didn't want to let my professor or his parents down. Then I would think what if I was making a mistake not liking him? He was everything I didn't like in a guy! Sooo clingy and whiny. A wonderfully nice man, but a complete doormat. He did everything I told him to do, like he was a little child. He would cry, afraid that I was going to leave him. I was insanely miserable. He sent me nice things in the mail. He bought me jewelry, shoes, clothes…He was a perfect gentleman, but I just wasn't attracted to anything about him whatsoever. I was in torment. I didn't want to hold his hand. It completely disgusted me. Stupid me kept trying to love him, because it seemed like the right thing to do. We, as women, can't allow ourselves to get trapped in this kind of situation. A lot of the time, if it looks right or feels right *(or it provides us with stability and security)* we **SETTLE**. Or maybe for you, it's the pressure from your friends and family that causes you to stay in relationships you know aren't right for you. **MAYBE** it's your pride. Never wanting everyone to know that something that looked good didn't work out.

I was stuck. He kept surprising me with amazing gifts, which made it even harder *(Don't judge me!)*. His parents began to plan our wedding, and I began to stress out even more. One day in particular, he was begging to play an app on my phone called *"Chicken Balls"*… this is where I snapped. I don't know if it was the whiny tone in his voice that was dragging out the word ballllls, or the fact that he wanted to get his hands on my phone to look through all my messages. All I know is…it drove me over the edge. We were actually in India at a conference I was performing at, when this incident occurred. Needless to say, I dumped him. This was not a smart move on my part, because now I was stuck in India for 3 more weeks with: him, his dad, my aggressive professor, and his brother! *"LET ME PLAY CHICKEN BALLLLLLS, VICTORIA!"* He whined in a super high pitched, girly voice that grossed me out to my core. *"Billy, we need to talk..."*, I whispered. We walked to the roof, and I let it all out. All the feelings I kept inside from everyone, while I was living this lie I thought I should be living. Of course he cried, and I sat there awkwardly until he was finished. What was even more horrible, is I didn't know he had arranged for us to have a 10 hour layover in Paris on our way back to the US, so he could get me flowers IN FREAKING PARIS! I felt like complete and utter crap after finding out he had gone to such lengths to surprise me. He began to tell me I was going against God's will, and tried to make me feel like I was rebelling against what God wanted. He arranged for me to meet with the professor who brought us together, so that maybe he could talk me into staying with him.

Don't let anyone manipulate you into doing something you know in your heart God doesn't want for you. You don't know how many times men have told me they are the one for me. I would have been married 5 times by the age of 25 if I would have settled for all those crazy dudes. Stay true to your feelings no matter what anyone says. Be patient while waiting for the one that's going to stop your heart. Just because someone looks good on the outside, and it looks like they've got everything together, doesn't mean you have to be with them.

I'll never know why my professor told me this guy was the guy God had for me, and I don't question his title as a Man of God. I still love and respect him with all of my heart. I believe that day in our class, he was picking up on the fact that I had come up for prayer for my husband; and he wanted to do his best to hook me up with a wonderful guy. It was my fault completely that I didn't let him know in the very beginning that I wasn't feeling anything at all. I was afraid I would miss an opportunity to be wealthy. I was afraid I would be alone forever. I was afraid of all sorts of stupid things. Fear will cause you to act crazy. Fear keeps you trapped in situations that feel uncomfortable. Stay true to your heart, and kick fear to the curb, so that you can live in freedom; not bound to other people's opinions of what your life should look like.

…While walking through the Paris airport *(after being in Paris close to 7 hours, with the guy I had dumped just a few weeks earlier)*, he asked, *"Can I at least get a kiss on the cheek?"* So I got on my tiptoes, and gave him the fastest kiss anyone had ever seen. I ask myself often, "Why didn't I end it sooner?!" I felt so horrible that I had to break the heart of this amazing guy, because I was too weak to stand up for what I knew was right.

7

TALK 15

Bad boys, Bad boys.

*B*AD BOYS, *it never gets easier to turn them down, you just become wiser, stronger, and more aware of what you deserve. You grow up.* **Grown women don't allow bad boys to waste their time.**

GOOD GIRLS *don't stoop down, our men* STEP UP!

He was so hot and mysterious and unlike chicken balls in every way…but baby, he was bad.

There he was, sitting on the fourth row beside a friend of mine, when I descended from the stage that Sunday morning. I had just sung my heart out at my father's church, and I felt confident as I took my seat. I was wearing a cute dress, heels, and was having a fantastic hair day, thank God. *"Who is that guy Bri is sitting next to? That boy is Fine!"*, I whispered to Raina. I kept glancing over at him hoping he wouldn't notice me staring. The entire service I wondered if he was taken or not. (I know. I know. I should've been paying attention in church.) I kept thinking to myself, *"Dang, I hope he's not dating Bri!"*

Finally, service was over. I slowly made my way to Bri and started a little small talk, hoping she would introduce me to her friend, but he had disappeared! *Dang it! Did he leave already?!* As I talked with Bri, a lady from the church barged in right between us with her newborn. She began to brag, show me pictures, and asked if I'd hold him for a

131

minute. I was thinking, *"Oh my goodness, this baby is cute, but I have to go find that handsome guy I had my eye on."* I scanned the crowd. There he was standing just a few feet behind the woman as she gabbed on. I caught his gaze. One subtle glance at this secretive man, and her words turned to mush in my ears. With a nod of his head and the slightest smile perched on the left side of his lips, he motioned me over. In the sexiest way possible, he screamed, "You're going to be mine, and you don't even know it yet.", without ever saying a word. My heart skipped a beat and I felt my stomach do something like a somersault. I, of course, did what I always do when I like a guy. I ignored him.

I looked back toward the nice lady, put on the prettiest smile I could muster, and continued talking to her, hoping that he was continuing to look at me. He sauntered over in a carelessly deliberate way that I had only seen actors in the movies do, tapped the nice lady on the shoulder, and asked to steal me for a moment. Why he bothered to ask then was beyond me, as I would quickly learn, asking was not something that he was in the habit of doing.

I was yet to look him directly in the eyes, afraid that I would appear as a deer-in-the-headlights, a scared baby deer spell-stricken and turned to stone. I handed the mother back her infant, and attempted to walk the short distance around to him without falling off of my heels. You know that feeling you get when a hot guy shows you some attention? It's like all of a sudden, you can't remember how to talk, let alone walk like a normal person *(especially in heels!)*. When I finally did, I noticed a certain familiarity about him. *Did I know him? Had I known him in another time?*

Familiarity turned to recognition as the gentle haze clouding my memory of him shifted. This was Thomas Black.

It was six years ago that we worked together at a small music shop downtown, Central City. It was cruddy and dark and carried an eclectic selection of music that you would be surprised that a girl like me had ever even heard of. It was the kind of place where my even being there drew on the classic question, *What's a girl like you doing in a place like this?*, and I think that's what I found most beautiful about it. We were teenagers then, and entirely too crossed, not by stars, but by station. Come to think of it, I was the only one who was a teenager then, and he was entirely too old, as I was entirely too indifferent, even put off by the cornrows in his hair and the tall tees that hung loosely on his thin body *(Not that there's anything wrong with that, it just wasn't my jam at the time; I was into punk rock drummers, unfortunately)*. Who would have guessed a guy with such an unmemorable place in my past, would have grown up to be such a tall, fine hunk of a man, and such an enigma in my immediate future?

I was awestruck. I turned to complete butter. And there I stood melting, like the Wicked Witch of the West, doused in liquid, for the whole church to see. Thomas Black had clearly grown up. Most men didn't have the guts to approach me, the reputable preacher's daughter, especially in front of my father and church family, unless they were complimenting my singing voice, or explaining how deeply touched they were by something I'd said over the microphone, like I was a cardboard cut out with a little talking speaker welded to the back of it, the perfect Little

Miss Christian trophy to be won by the first Mr. Christian Ken Doll that could hold my attention. Thomas Black was different. Thomas didn't see me as the notoriously untouchable, *virgin in charge* like everyone else, but as the young girl he sold records alongside many years before, whose personality and wit won him over way back when, before he ever realized I was ever anyone's role model or *favorite worship leader*. He saw me, the real me, without all the churchy hype, and I loved it.

More importantly, dang, he had gotten SUPER FINE over the years! His sexy, fresh fade and his perfectly trimmed beard around his kissable lips made you wanna scream, *"Thank you, Jesus, for the fade!"* He was smooth, seductive and oh, so confident! His big brown eyes made you feel like he could melt your heart with one single look. I, of course, gave my number away to those eyes, and there you have it; and there he had me. The wicked attraction began its course, and off we went bound for destruction.

I remember the first time we were alone like it was last night. I stood outside at the end of our long driveway, waiting safely out of the view of my father's eyes. It was close to ten as the summer sun had already fallen below the horizon of the open fields my house sits upon. I looked to my right, and the air was black. At the sound of a low rumbling I shifted my gaze to the left to see his yellow high beam lights cutting through the otherwise still dark. He pulled up close to me, and I definitely slid into his black Chevrolet Camaro 1SS. I fastened my seatbelt, like any good girl would, looked over at him quizzically and he asked if I wanted to take a stroll.

It was warm that night in Kentucky. The mosquitos were thick, but we didn't care. We would've endured a lot worse just to be near one another. I remember thinking to myself while we had driven to the nearest park, *"This will just be a fun, short-lived fling. I'm not going to let myself really like this guy."* As we walked the trail he was quiet and mysterious. I wanted to know every thought he was thinking. He listened tolerantly as I rambled on about my dreams for the future, and all I was believing God to do. There's nothing like a man that can patiently listen! *DANG!* Anyway, we came upon a big hill, and I remember letting out a very quiet sigh. Before I could even tell him to *get his hands off of me,* he had quickly scooped me up and thrown me across his shoulders like I weighed nothing but a few pounds, then proceeded to to run up the hill like he was a freaking Navy Seal! I think in that very moment I fell into deep *lust* with him. Ha! I'm such a credulous sucker! After releasing me from his arms, he immediately, without requesting permission, grabbed my face and kissed me long and hard. I was flabbergasted. I loved that he wasn't afraid to touch me or take control, but my love for his "boldness" *(if you want to call it that)* wouldn't be a good thing in just a short couple of weeks. He wasn't afraid of me in the slightest. By the end of the walk I had fallen for him, hard. I distinctly remember the moment it really hit me. He was opening my car door. I looked up at him after I sat in the passenger seat, and there it was… Some people may call it love. It was most likely lust, but nonetheless, I was ALL UP IN IT!

Who would have known at the age of 22, I would be

more tempted to give in to temptation than ever before. It's always the people you least expect, and it's always at the most surprising of times. I had been home from Bible College for close to a year then, and boy, did I think I had it all together. I wasn't looking to start another unhealthy relationship. In my perfect world, I was ready to get married, and I wasn't going to get involved with anyone because of immature loneliness or foolish lust. I thought I was at my strongest. I was wrong.

What started out as a casual thing turned into something far more serious with this mysterious bad boy, something that completely consumed my heart and soul. I began to lie to my parents about where I was going, so that I could sneak off with him to have long hardcore makeout sessions. Time started to fly by so fast that I couldn't keep track. I was spiraling downward, falling into the forbidden abyss. I was falling in love, but with someone that had no business dominating my life. I gave into my weakness for him countless times, and came so close to losing my virginity. I thought if I changed for him, maybe he would change for me, but the more I gave in to him, the more he held on to his crazy lifestyle. I found out he was dealing marijuana and had multiple children by different women, one of them being raised in my own hometown! At first, I was disgustingly heart-broken by everything I was finding out about him, but he always had a way of calming me down, and manipulating me to get me back in his good graces. Covering up his lies, allowing things to go way too far sexually, and horrible fights were a normal part of my life now. It was so very hard for me to get away from this toxic relationship, and I didn't even know why! *(Duh, sexual addictions)* I knew in my heart he wasn't the one, but I continued to let it keep going. I didn't have the strength to say goodbye to him. I was addicted to his attention. It always amazes me that when we think we are at our strongest, God will be quick to reveal how badly we are in need of Him.

I remember walking out of my house late one summer night, when my father stopped me and said, *"Tori, you've come this far, don't get this close and give up now."* He didn't have to say anymore, I knew what He was referring to. I was so very close to giving it all up for this guy. I wanted sex so badly! I can't thank God enough for keeping me safe, and giving me the strength not to allow it to go too far. It was a difficult test to walk through and I pray it was my last.

At first, I honestly didn't think for one second that Thomas was going to be such a bad influence on me. He was a nice, sweet guy who seemed to treat me very well. I had no idea he was doing things that were totally against everything that I believed in and lived for, like selling large amounts of weed and distributing his sperm to the entire city. Here's the catch: I knew in my heart something wasn't right, but because he gave me butterflies, I ignored God's voice in my head, and told myself, "I'll be fine. I won't really fall for him...no...not me!" That's how it always begins...*Talk to him just a little bit...Kiss him just a little bit...Lift up your skirt just a little bit.* Well, there I was giving a little bit, and a little bit more and little did I know that for over two years I would be tormented by my attraction for this man; and, it was entirely my fault.

I remember standing in my driveway late one night, after letting him go for good. It ended right where it started, as I watched his taillights grow smaller and smaller in the distance, until they couldn't be seen at all. I felt my Jesus so close to me, and I heard Him say, *"Hi, babygirl... I've got your back."* In that moment I've never felt more loved. I've never felt more complete. I was so proud of myself, because I knew He was proud of me. That is the key right there...if you want to feel self worth - bury yourself in Jesus and in His ways. He is the only one who will give you true worth and purpose. There is nothing quite like the love of the Father. His love is perfect. *There is no fear in love. But perfect love drives out fear, because fear has to do with punishment. The one who fears is not made perfect in love. We love because HE FIRST loved us. 1 John 4:18-19* **We were created to be satisfied by Him.** Jesus is jealous over us, and won't allow us to be entangled with someone, who is literally tearing our souls apart from Him. He will put a stop to it if we can't. When Jesus steps in, you and everybody around you better watch out. No one messes with *God's girl.* When you truly experience a small taste of Him, it makes every sexy bad boy in the world look like the most unattractive punk ever! Please do not get to the point where I was. End it before your heart and soul is invested.

Let the morning bring me word of your unfailing love, for I have put my trust in you. Show me the way I should go, for to you I entrust my life. Psalm 143:8

This is how God showed his love among us: He sent His one and only Son into the world that we might live through Him. This is love: not that we loved God, but that He loved us and sent His Son as an atoning sacrifice for our sins. 1 John 4:9-10

We all have one thing in common. We are women who like men. We probably all have a few things we could share, when it comes to past stories of dating and heartbreak. I, myself, have acted very crazy at times, and I'm sure you have as well. I have left my morals behind and have forgotten the promises I made to God. Despite my desire to remain spotless, I would time and time again find myself wrapped around the wrong men. This is why I am writing this book. I'm sick of seeing people, like myself, fall into the same 'ole traps that the enemy has laid out for us. He tricks us with them almost every time. (*Enters cute boy, with what we think is "swagger" and wit, he shows us some attention, we fall for him, and suddenly he treats us like crap! BAM, just like that...we are hooked!*) If we aren't lucky enough to get away, our precious time with our bad boy will turn into a failed attempt at romance; leaving us alone once again.

Do not be deceived: "Bad company corrupts good morals."

I Corinthians 15:33

Don't be fooled! It can be extremely wrong, when it feels very good. (STD's come later, now those don't feel so great... so I've heard.)

When we merge ourselves with the bad boy, we are emotionally killing ourselves. Let's face it - he is never going to be the man we want him to be. Yet, we are found caught with our legs open, indulging and obsessing over a man, who has no right touching us in the first place.

Here are a few thoughts I have as to why I may have fallen for the bad boy quite a few times. *I feel that maybe I usually like them because they are tough, a little on the rough side, and in need of nurturing.* As a woman, God created me to be nurturing. I'm not attracted to a man that has a softer, more delicate personality than myself. I want him to tell me how it is and put me in my place. I want him to lead me.

In my personal experiences, a lot of guys who aren't necessarily the *"bad boy"* type, have appeared to be overly sensitive. I'm in no way saying that, every good guy is overly emotional and whimpy. That would be an extremely idiotic thing for me to think. I'm just telling you about my encounters with guys and how I've perceived them. I've come across many church boys, who I've seen crumble and diminish under the tough criticism of their beliefs. Many times they would speak badly about their own churches, and the churches they were involved with, and the Pastors they served under - on our dates! Unfortunately, so many church men I have tried to be with, were not fully committed to their faith. *I hated that.* I wanted to see them changing the world, because of their conviction and love for Jesus; and not become weak and go back on what they believed in. Sometimes I've felt as if they were too afraid to pursue me, in fear they would feel emasculated. Mostly because of my affection for ministering the word of God - through preaching and praise and worship.

Bad boys have never had any trouble approaching me, and letting me know that I am what they want. That always attracted me to them. *I have allowed myself to fall for the wrong men, because there seemed to be a lack of strong men with conviction, inside my churches.* I want someone to grab me when I'm crying about my dreams being crushed, and with passion and vigor, remind me of what God is going to do in my life! I envision him picking me up and kissing me to calm me down, until I regained my composure.

Bad boys gave me the tough love that I craved, but it wasn't the right kind of love. It wasn't healthy. I wasn't finding what I needed in the church, so I found myself settling for men outside of the church.

An overly sensitive guy, to me, is like an avocado that's just a little too ripe. If you squeeze too hard, it will bruise and become ruined. I need a coconut kind of guy, so I can be as strong willed as I want and know that he's gonna hold up in Godly confidence. A guy who won't break no matter the storm. Where are you, coconut guy?!

Have you ever noticed that when you begin to fool around with the wrong guy, your emotions become screwed up, and you are suddenly unable to focus on anything but him. Pleasing him. Being with him. Changing him into the man you want him to be begins to consume your life, and suddenly you are wrapped up in toxic passion. Maybe you have never gone this far sexually with anyone else before. Now you've created a soul tie with this person, and your emotions become deeply rooted in them.

If you want to be successful in any aspect of life, a bad boy is the worst thing for your drive and ambition. Why, because suddenly the wrong person is the first priority in your life. You may think you can keep him at bay, but you are only fooling yourself. His kisses will be too sweet to stay away from, and before you know it, your panties will be slipping off. We must reclaim our independence, our strength, and our ambition! Don't let anyone, especially someone who is just going to bring you down, stand in the way of your dream! You only have one life to live, don't waste it on people who don't matter in the long run. People who aren't living their lives with purpose. We can help them yes - encourage them yes - show them the love of Jesus, absolutely...but we can't have sex with them!

If the devil can't ruin your young years with: drugs, alcohol, self-abuse, partying... he will use the wrong relationship to get you off track. He wants your young years to be wasted! He wants to keep you distracted! Don't let his lies be the reason you don't catch your breath until the age 35! Your youth was meant for discovering who you are in Christ. It's meant for dreaming. When you are young, you are afforded the opportunity to fall in love with Jesus. You don't have all the stress that adulthood brings. More than anything else, the enemy wants to steal those years from you because they are some of the most important years of your life! These are the years that shape your future. These years build a strong foundation for all that is to come in your life. If you are consumed with a bad relationship, you can't figure out what you really even need in your life. You can't decipher what you even want in life! You can't build a strong relationship with Jesus if all you think about is how you can get your parents out of the house, so you can bang what's his name!

How can a young man keep his way pure? By guarding it according to YOUR word. Psalm 119:9

Bad boys usually come with a chase.

<u>*Why do we love the chase?*</u>

1. We want what we think we can't have *(what's unattainable is sexy and adventurous)*

2. It's the thing to do, because he's the guy everyone wants *(Nobody is waiting outside all night for the new Wal-Mart brand kicks)*

3. We want to feel accepted by someone that isn't so accepting of our *"good girl"* persona.

4. He reminds us of someone who has rejected us in the past, and catching him might erase some of that pain.

5. It's a game that we do not want to lose, because it will hurt our pride.

6. We want to look like the desired bad-a$$ among our peers.

7. We want to be the girl he changes everything for.

It will be easy to obtain their *D*, but difficult to secure their heart. We always want what we don't have, or better yet, what we can't have. Usually, the kind of man we can't get to commit to us, are most likely the bad ones. Why, because a relationship doesn't matter to them. He's either sperming up the whole dang neighborhood, or consumed by the party lifestyle. He pops up when he wants our attention, *(aka when he's horny)* and then he disappears. We want the bad boy, because he's mysterious and fun to talk to our friends about. We want him, because we want to be the first one to change his bad boy ways, and that makes us feel validated as women. We want him because he's more sexually experienced than the good guy and that's SO hot. *(Your vagina is also going to be hot if you keep messing with him - while he's inside everyone else)* He's a thrill. He's an exciting turn from our peaceful Christian existence.

I could go on and on about the different reasons why we may keep falling for the bad boy...or the controlling guy...or the whine-bag or the bum. I have my reasons and you have yours. What we need to start doing is focus on the value we place on our bodies and our hearts. Why can't we wait on the good guy, who turns us on just like the bad boy does. You could be ruining your chances with the sexy guy that worships God with all his heart, because you are obsessed with the bad boy waiter that turns you on. Don't be caught in this game. Once you are caught in this game the bad boy has for you, there is no getting out! *(at least for a long while)* It will never end well. Trust in God enough to know that He knows what you're attracted to. He knows exactly the kind of man you want and He has someone that is perfectly designed with your tastes in mind. God is not stupid. He knows what will turn you on. Trust in Him! We can't let the bad boy distract us and keep us off course. Satan, *(the guy that wants to keep every good thing God has for you, far away from you)* will ALWAYS send you the bad boy, to keep you distracted from the man you are truly waiting for, a Godly man.

The fear of man lays a snare, but whoever trusts in the Lord is safe. Proverbs 29:25

Commit your way to the Lord; trust in Him, and He will act. Psalm 37:5

Blessed is the man who trusts the Lord. Jeremiah 17:7

The Lord will rescue me from any evil deed and bring me safely into His kingdom. 2 Timothy 4:18

Be strong and courageous. Do not be frightened, and do not be dismayed, for the Lord your God is with you wherever you go. Joshua 1:9

So how do we stop falling for these men? These men

who are chipping away at our character? We have to stop it before it begins. We have to pay attention to the signs, ladies. Let's get old school for a second. Make him take you on a date, before you allow him to slip his hand under your skirt! Test him out, see if he has the tendency to become controlling, when you say you are busy for the night and can't talk for a while. See if he becomes crazy jealous, when you mention one of your guy friends. We have to have strategic war plans, if we are going to succeed in love. It is way too easy to fall in love with the wrong guy, and it is just as easy to settle.

Why do we as women expect these men to be something they're not! It's our **OWN** stupid fault for giving them our precious time. I was giving so much of my emotion and body to a man who didn't deserve it. Jesus didn't deserve it either…and neither did my close friend, Landon. *(who I didn't know was going to **die** from a drug overdose, while I was consumed with this **bad boy**.)* Wow, look at what the enemy will do to you! He had me so distracted. I didn't even notice my own friend was dying. You have no idea the pain and guilt I felt for ignoring my friend the way I did. I should have been there for him. I should've gone to where he was when he needed me most! When reality hits you like it did me when I got the call that my beloved Landon was DEAD, you realize who's truly worth your time and who's not REAL QUICK!

The thief comes only to steal, kill, and destroy; I have come that they may have life, and have it to the full. John 10:10

146

Bury yourself in passion that pushes you to a better life with Jesus.

If you are not his priority why do you think he deserves to be YOURS?

The older I become, the more I run into bad boys that are completely used to wrecking every girl that peaks their interest. The thought of an actual real life good girl is unbelievable to them. Let me tell you another story, just a quickie.

A few years ago, I reunited with an old friend of mine named Travis. He had some extremely rough times when we were kids. In the past ten years, his successful bodybuilding father suffered a brain aneurysm, and lost all of his brain function. He couldn't move, speak, or convey any emotion. Travis, who was one of the smartest people I've ever known, was forced to quit school and take care of his father. It became too much for him. He started drinking alcohol, and taking drugs. I felt so very bad for him. I began to invite him to friendly functions, and to church on Sunday. At first, I was trying to steer him in the right direction. I wanted to introduce him to Godly people, who were also having fun in life. I wanted him to see that he didn't have to party like a crazy animal or shoot heroin to forget about his problems. I wanted to introduce him to the way I lived, a Godly life that was still full of fun. This guy's looks made it difficult for me to stay focused though. This dude was **HOT!** I mean like movie-star **HOT!** I mean like he walks in a room and all the girls start starring,

HOT! I remember one particular night, I invited him over with a crew of my friends to watch a movie. As soon as he walked in the room, we could smell alcohol on his breath. He wasn't himself, but I didn't say anything. After everyone had gone home for the night, I was left alone with my friend Travis. He was knocked out on the couch like he was under anesthesia. I didn't know what to do. He had his head propped up on his hand. So I gently creped over and knocked his hand out from under his face, in hopes it would wake him up! His hand fell to his side and he remained asleep. At this point, I'm cracking up. How was I going to wake him up? I wanted him out of my house! I said a small prayer under my breath, *"Jesus, please wake Travis up, and please Lord, don't let him overdose right in front of me."* Shortly after the prayer he actually woke up! Thank God! I walked him to the door and suddenly, without any warning, he kissed me! Shockingly, it was a very good kiss. I liked the kiss. What in the world was wrong with me! By the way, he smoked 2 packs of cigarettes a day, so, I tell myself that's a *HUGE NO GO* for me and it's completely disgusting. I would never date someone who smoked that much, let alone allow them to kiss me. It's amazing how fast and easy a girl can go back on her word, when a boy is just so darn good looking. So there it began. Fast forward to a few weeks later, after we had become pretty close to one another. He had taken me on quite a few dates, attended church with me multiple times, and even hung out with my family. One night he was driving me home, and he mentioned something about sex. I quickly told him that I was a virgin. He looked at me in total shock. He was absolutely stunned. I remember him saying, *"What!? Are you kidding me? We need to go to my house right now and fix this!"* I laughed and told him that this was a decision I made a long time ago. Keeping my virginity was actually something I was proud of. He couldn't believe what I was saying and just kept ranting in disgust. *"Girls actually wait to have sex? Why would anyone want to do that? It's not healthy! It's not normal!"* he said. The more he went on, the more I became very angry and hurt. I had never had anyone react this way when I told them why I was waiting to have sex. He looked at me like I was a freak. I knew then and there I could not let him take me on any more dates, and I should never have let his lips touch mine. *Gag!* I was meant to help my friend not make out with him.

You are the light of the world. A town built on a hill cannot be hidden. Neither do people light a lamp and put it under a bowl. Instead they put it on it's stand, and it gives light to everyone in the house. In the same way, let your light shine before others, that they may see your good deeds and glorify your Father in heaven. Matthew 5:14-16

Quit making out with the people God has called you to help. Instead, lead them to the only one who has hope and peace for them, Jesus. It hit me so hard one day when my brother said, *"Tori, Travis doesn't need a girlfriend he needs someone to lead him to Jesus right now."* Suddenly I realized how selfish I was being! All because I wanted to kiss somebody for a few minutes, and go on a few dates. *(because I was lonely)* I could be ruining my chance to be what I was actually called to be in this guy's life! Not to mention, this guy was pressuring me hardcore to have sex with him! He's never even heard of people not having sex at my age! HAHA!

BREAKDOWN MOMENT! How many Horny Toads do I have to kiss, before I find my prince? It feels as if I'm drying up like a prune. The wait is almost too much. Am I a freak because I want to hold on to my virginity? Sometimes these questions haunt me, especially after coming in contact with certain people of the male persuasion.

Sometimes people will tear you down, for what you have decided to stand for. You can't let it derail you. Good girls can have fun and abstain from sex. Good girls can be sexy and still remain pure. We are who **real men** want! Who cares about the horny little boys that may make fun of our mature decisions.

The Wait - The Struggle

I sat alone in my beautifully decorated bedroom. The candles were burning, and fireflies were shining a dim light on the bedroom wall through the windows. It was Christmas night. The day had been filled with absolute joy. I received every gift I could ever ask for, and my family was once again together and completely happy. Yet, there I was sitting alone on Christmas night, 24 years old about to turn 25. The thought made me cringe. I remember feeling overwhelmed and thinking to myself, *"I have so much I want to accomplish before I turn 30! I have to birth five kids, start up orphanages in Africa, and tell an entire generation of people that Jesus has a purpose for their lives!"* I felt as if I was running out of time. All the ignorant boys that have consumed my life for the past few years, were a trap set up by Satan, and I walked right into it. I felt, in this moment, very ashamed of myself. I was broken-hearted. Not because of my last drawn out relationship, but because of my own stupidity to allow it to happen.

At this time, I had recently met quite an incredible man, who to my *GREAT* surprise, sent me flowers and took me on a wonderful date. He was the kind of man that had the potential to be *"the one."* I stalked his social media like a preteen freak. My friend had recently gone through my internet history looking for a website, and was completely ashamed to see his name everywhere. Now I had the sudden urge to look up his recent Instagram photo and kiss the screen on my iPhone. Gulp… Sorry, let's get back to talking about waiting.

I thought maybe my waiting had come to a halt, when I received those flowers a few weeks earlier. I was just beginning to learn that my waiting had just begun. This was a whole new level of trusting in God. This was the kind of waiting you would do without the side guys. The kind of waiting I should have been doing for the last 7 years.

God spoke to me before I knew this wonderfully photogenic god of a man was interested in me. He told me to get rid of all the guys in my life, that I was basically playing games with to fill up my *"lonely time."* I tried my best, but I still was not completely there yet. I would get weak and give into a text here and there. The photogenic god was now in another country for a month, and it has been extremely hard to stay away from other guys who tempt me. I want you to understand it is not that I'm having sex with them or even making out with them. For some odd reason I crave their attention to brighten my day. I was simply bored. I know God spoke to me to get rid of these guys, because I needed to start preparing myself for the man He had for me. So I got myself together, and deleted all their numbers! I told them I was done with the games, and said I couldn't see them anymore. Almost as soon as I had done it, this handsome on fire for God preaching model sent me the most beautiful bouquet of flowers! He secretly found out that my favorite color was purple, so they were all shades of purple. After receiving the flowers I thought, *"Dang God, you work fast!"* Then it started to go slow. What started out, as a very exciting communication between the two of us, turned very stagnant. I started to wonder if I wasn't good enough. As he became increasingly distant, it became harder to stay away from all the side guys I had previously deleted. In the end it didn't work out with the photogenic god of a man. Even still, I'm so very glad God taught me what He did. I feel like God was telling me that, at any time HE could bring into my life whoever He wanted, and that He wanted me to be strong enough to stay away from all the wrong men. I learned that I could let go of the side dudes, and give my full attention to what God was showing me at the time. I learned to conquer loneliness and the need for constant attention.

Maybe you are in a similar situation where you know in your heart, the one you're messing around with; isn't the perfect fit for you. Yet, you still fool around, because you are too weak to be alone. We must love ourselves enough to let go of the wrong people and endure our loneliness, with strength and courage. Love yourself enough to be lonely for the time being. **The wait and the loneliness will vanish in an instant when 'he' finds you, and you will be so proud you were able to stand on your own.**

He gives strength to the weary and increases the power of the weak. Even the youths grow tired and weary, and young men stumble and fall; but those who hope in the Lord will renew their strength. they will soar on wings like eagles; they will run and not grow weary. They will walk and not be faint. Isaiah 40:29-31

TALK 17

Fake Reality

It helped that he was a Kentucky boy - that always helps. I first met him while hanging with this cocky musician friend of mine, who I was kind of sort of dating at the time. What really drew me in was his sarcasm and interesting way of communicating. He was also a little mean in a sexy way. *(DING! Revelation)* When I realized the cocky musician, who thought he was God's gift to the female race, was nothing but a gross little player; I felt I had permission to be even more interested in his sarcastic friend, James. It also helped my ego to get back at the little player! *(Guys hate when you call them little ☺ take that!)* Ladies, don't lie, I know you've used the word *"little"* to get back at a guy!

In time, this mild adventurous attraction turned into something far more important, and I never once saw it coming. It's hard for me to describe, because I am still *(to this very day)* unaware of why this man had me so captivated by him and why it went on for as long as it did.

We were complete opposites in every way. I like to go against the grain, which is probably why I liked him. It's my rebellious and stubborn nature that keeps me hung up on guys that aren't very good for me. I like to argue. I like to shock people and make them think. This is a blessing, as well as a curse. *(be careful that your God given abilities and quirks are giving you life and not death)*

I became very attached in a short period of time. We just clicked. I'm not 100% sure how I became this way with someone via text...all I know is that when you attach yourself to someone for a long enough period of time, most likely - you will fall into some kind of love with them. In this case, for me, it was fake love in a fake reality and I fell hard.

As I was moving out of Chicago, he was moving in, which was a very good thing. Girl, if we had been in the same city at the same time, we most likely would have done some damage to my morals. *(only mine because he didn't have any)* I don't remember exactly how we first began talking after I had moved. He helped fix my computer at the Apple store once while I still lived in the city. *(which is probably where he stole my number now that I think about it.)* How romantic! Such a *LITTLE* bad boy. I used to have a thing for guys that fixed computers. *(only the Father up above knows why)* He was weird in the sense that he didn't care what anyone thought of him, and he freely expressed his opinions. I could tell he was intelligent by the way he spoke and the words he would use. That piqued my interest. He was sarcastic, witty, and seemed to be very confident. **CONFIDENCE** is key! He had my full attention, which doesn't happen often. Especially for as long as this went on. *(Unfortunately, I think I have GUY A.D.D.)* To become so interested in someone via text, is something else I have never understood. It's something I use to make fun of other girls for doing it. Like, really, how can you dig a guy you don't see? I have never liked anyone like him, maybe that was a *"turn on"* I suppose. He was interested in my good girl behavior *(in the beginning)*, and I loved that about him...but it didn't last.

We began to talk...a lot. I soon began to talk to him more than I talked to anyone else, and I didn't know why! He was like my escape from reality. He was the only person that I talked to that didn't change the way they spoke, just because it was me; *(and I worked in ministry)* or tried to act over spiritual in my presence. He was very real and I could be real with him. He was my comfort in this crazy hectic world I lived in, and in a sense he was my drug, my relaxation.

It baffles me how one could become so hung up on something that was 100% cyber! I imagine it was the fact that he was a real human being on the other end of the text...and the fact that I had met him quite a few times in person helped as well. We were 10 hours apart and it somehow felt real. *(maybe it was - maybe it wasn't. THIS IS WHY YOU CAN'T MAKE DECISIONS solely on FEELINGS alone! Feelings can be terrible leaders)*

After a year or so, I began to build this picture in my mind of what I wanted him to be for me, and what I wanted in the future; whether it was actually possible didn't matter to me. It was comforting having him *"around"*, and that's all that mattered. I dreamt of spending real time with him and falling in love. I wanted our story to be this grand adventure that no one expected or saw coming. In my mind he was there for me, and that really made me think it was real. *(BUT IT WAS ALL A DREAM!)* What makes this even more interesting, is, the entire time he had a whole life I didn't know about. *Just wait...*

We were having a conversation once and I said, *"Man, these kids around here are poppin' out babies like nothing I've ever seen!"* He then told me he was going to have a daughter in a few months. **WAIT! WHAT?!** Don't you just love it when men slide those huge details in like that? Like they are going to get by with it. I was like, *"Ummm, who's the mama and where is she at, sir?"* He assured me that she wasn't in the picture and that he would do everything he could to take care of his child. So, for some reason I let it go, and continued talking to him.

I couldn't let James go for some reason! I was so used to telling him about everything in my day, and simply talking to him about whatever was upsetting me. I liked to share my frustrations and emotions with him, because he wasn't in my world. I am usually in a position of leadership, and it's hard to find people you can simply just talk to about real life. *(Who is your go to person? And are they a healthy influence in your life?)*

It was a pretty chill day at the *Rich* crib, where my intern and I were working on a few things, when I suddenly received a phone call with the same area code as this sexy preacher man I was currently talking to at the time. I asked Raina to QUICKLY pick it up and answer it as my intern. *(I just wanted to look cool - FAIL)* She answers, *"Hello, Victoria Rich's office."* *(Tsk tsk. We giggled)* Suddenly, I hear a screaming female on the other end of the phone! *"LET ME (BLEEPING) TALK TO VICTORIA. RIGHT (BLEEPING) NOW!"* My eyes grew bigger than usual, and my heart was racing at this point. *"Who the heck is this?"* Raina asked. *"This is James' (BLEEPING) baby mama!"* (she said with a sarcastic tone probably, because that's what I called her when James and I would talk about the situation) So, I grabbed the phone and said: *"Hello, who is this?"* *"THIS IS (BLEEPING) ABBY!"* I knew who it was but I acted dumb. *"Ummmmm, who???"* I said in my best ghetto white girl voice. She then began to scream at me conversations that James and I recently had. Some of them weren't very good conversations. I began to sweat instantly. My eyes look over at Raina and she looks horrified. *(Like I have said before, I get horny too, I love Jesus but unfortunately, I haven't been perfect. Sometimes I want to talk about other things besides my 5-year plan and 10 steps to financial success. I have messed up big time and many, many times...)* ANYWAY, this girl was screaming at me, and Raina could hear her every word; because the stupid volume on my phone was all the way up! My poor intern, whom I was supposed to be an example for can hear all of this crazy embarrassing crap! Man, crazy females can really make my blood boil. I quickly turn down the volume on my iPhone and walk away. *"I'll be right back ☺."* I walked downstairs and tried to calm this girl down. She began to tell me that James was in Texas on business, and he left his iPad at the house. She then told me that she has read **EVERYTHING** we have ever talked about! *(DUDE, you don't know how to work the delete function!)* For some reason she turns into an emotional female, and begins to have this weird heart to heart with me. *"Listen! I just found out I have an STI, because he let a random chick give him head and of course he came and had sex with me afterwards!*

Now I have an STI!" she screamed/cried. I was in shock. I had no idea what to say. I felt like the most ignorant person on the planet. Even to this day I think back and it terrifies me for some reason. To think that I really bought into his crap, is what scares me the most. Anyway, I went all sugary sweet on her and told her I would be praying for her family, and I hoped they could work everything out. MY LIFE HAS BEEN CRAZY! Oh, and by the way, she assured me that if I didn't back off, she was going to post our conversations all over the Internet! I assured her that I never wanted to speak to his nasty behind again, and that I had no freaking clue she lived with him and that they were still together. I felt horrible for her. I feel horrible for every other female on the planet that has to go through situations like this.

My mom used to say, *"Your sin will find you out.",* and boy, was she right... I messed up. Enough said.

If you're wondering about Raina, I apologized to the poor girl for being such a bad example. I explained to her what I've been explaining to you, that although I am a follower and lover of Jesus, I am not perfect and I screw up... a lot. We laughed about it for hours and all was forgiven. HUGE LESSON LEARNED.

Wake up and look at what is real around you, what God has *on purpose* placed in your life. There are people in your world that can help you get to new heights in your creativity, wisdom, and relationships. Lean on those people. Don't waste your time on someone who won't help you fall in love with Jesus even more. If they aren't pulling you closer to God, God didn't place them in your life

- Satan did. I'm not saying everyone in your world has to be saved or perfect. All I'm saying is, if you realize the relationship is provoking you to do things that are pulling you further away from God, they were sent to you by Satan. God doesn't send people in your life to tempt you or purposely cause you to screw up. He always sets you up to win.

Why do we hold on to people for years that are in no way benefiting our lives? What provokes us to become addicted to people who hold no promise for our future. Security? Loneliness? Lust? Boredom? Insecurity? Weakness? Look in the mirror and recognize it... then suffocate it with the presence of God. Woman, you carry the future of the world inside you.

Suffocate your weakness with the presence of God and watch how strength will overtake your obstacles.

Penis + Priorities

Purity > Penis

We would rather get a text from a guy, than a word from God. How did our priorities get so messed up? Why do we feel our worth comes from that call he makes to us at midnight - just to tell us he's horny? Why is it that a text from him in the morning is the only thing that starts our day off right? Why is it that we'll suck on his jimmy, just to make him stay for a few more weeks?

As women we need to feel loved, protected, desirable, and let's face it - we want to feel sexy. Sometimes these needs that God has put in us, can turn into weakness, because we aren't placing them in the proper place or time. We become desperate for the stability that a man gives us, not realizing that God is the only one who can give us true security and love. I've seen girls do almost anything to feel desired by the opposite sex. We will give up our virginity that we've held on to for so long just to feel loved by one boy that doesn't even treat us right, or isn't even close to being the one God has designed for us. We must become aware of our needs and bury them in Jesus. He is the only one who will make us feel completely desired and loved. He is the only one who can love us the way we deserve to be loved. Quit taking off your panties for boys, who only want you for the 15 second orgasm he wants to achieve. Quit allowing them to touch you in areas - only your husbands were meant to touch! Quit pushing away the husband whom you haven't met yet, prolonging this journey of waiting. Your husband is going to greatly appreciate the sacrifices you are getting ready to start making!

SOUND THE ALARM! If a man attempts to sleep with you on the first date, the first week, the first month or - EVER; *(when he knows you are trying to save yourself for marriage)* then he is a pig! Cook that Pig for breakfast, and then throw him out like last week's trash! Why do I compare men to food? Well, frankly because, men and food are a lot alike. We sometimes do not want to consume what's good and healthy for us. We mostly reach for the greasy potato chips, because it's easy, tastes good, and gives us instant satisfaction. We aren't willing to take the 20 extra minutes - to cook something that would be beneficial to our body, and give us more strength in the long run. This is how we are with men sometimes! We meet someone that looks real good on the outside, and kisses very well, yet we know they aren't husband material, but because it's in front of us *(and it feels so dang good)* we begin to give this guy our full attention. We aren't willing to wait on the premium meat, are we ladies?! It's almost as if we don't have any trust in God. We have to look past the here and now, and see with the eyes of God. Lay down the potato chips and wait patiently for the broccoli to finish steaming!

Your future awaits you. Lay aside every weight (or man) that may have you down in the dirt, and start running toward the life God has for you. We can do it. We will wait.

What if we pursued God the way we pursue sex, men, and marriage? Where would we be? Who would we be?

Allow me to dream for a second. If I had completely trusted God with - knowing who to bring into my life and when throughout these past years, I wouldn't have messed with guys I knew weren't right for me. If I would have been more focused on helping YOU and less focused on helping the men who were detouring me from my purpose and call *(while making out with me)* I probably would have finished this book 5 years ago! If I would have put Jesus where he belongs in my life, on the throne, I would be so in love and filled with his presence that people could feel Him immensely when I walked beside them. I suspect I would probably have seen and expected more miracles, because my eyes would be completely fixed on Jesus as He built my faith stronger and stronger, as He took me from glory to glory! I would be far more free to dream and believe, for I wouldn't be bound by the fear of loneliness. I wouldn't have to fight against sexual demons that have attached themselves to me through my past situations and soul ties. I could be anywhere I wanted in this life with Jesus... instead of obsessing why I'm still alone or how I can secure a MAN.. I would simply be waiting, and trusting in my God, my King.

Wait on the Lord and He will renew your strength. Isaiah 40:31

I have some really good news for you though. GOD DOES NOT WASTE ANY OF OUR TIME! Even the time you think was wasted because of all your bad mistakes will be used for your good. Yes, I could've done a lot of things differently. But, this is my story. These were my weaknesses. We ALL have faults. We all have a story. BECAUSE I'VE BEEN WILLING TO SHARE my story with you God has grown me in ways I never thought possible, and hopefully you've allowed Him to grow you while reading. (I've been a fearful girl almost all my life, afraid of not pleasing people. Look at me telling all my dirty secrets to the world in total freedom!)

God is good. I really mean that. It's that simple. He never gives up on us. He is never disappointed or ready to give up on our lives. He loves us with a love that can not go away. It's not even in His nature to be unloving. He is love. He's been waiting for you to simply realize these things and run to Him. He wants to wipe you clean from all the heartache, all the filthy mistakes. He wants to begin to walk with you on this journey.

They triumphed over Him by the blood of the Lamb and by the word of their testimony. Revelation 12:11

And we know that all things work together for good to those who love God, to those who are called according to His purpose. Romans 8:28

...God is love. 1 John 4:8

Good Girl, you are who Jesus wants. You are His greatest desire. You are His prize; His bride. His greatest possession. He's been pursuing you since you took your first breath. Thousands of years before you were even born He died so that you could live a life with Him free of sin or bondage. No matter the depth or height of the mistakes you have made HE SEES YOU PURE, because He has covered you in His blood which wipes it all away. He sees the woman you will be when you have let go of all the baggage that weighs you down, and that is the woman He has created you to be. He's ready to go to war for you AND HE HAS ALREADY WON THE GREATEST BATTLE ON THE CROSS! He's building you a mansion in Heaven and waits for the day to spend all of eternity lavishing you in His love. With Him by your side you can not fail. It is impossible. Say, YES! Run into His arms and start again, or maybe for the first time! NOW is the time!

God spoke these words to me while I was writing this, *"If you can conquer it, I'll show you the world."* He says the same to you. *"It"* for me, was a few things. He knew *it* - I knew *it,* and they have been **CONQUERED** in Jesus name.

There is absolutely nothing you cannot do when you have Jesus in the forefront of your life. Join me and so many others as we continue to pursue purity. Join us on this adventure to wait. I'm not saying this road will be easy. As a matter of fact, it will be harder than you ever imagined, but together we can do this! Welcome to the Good Girl Movement.

You are more powerful than you even know. Go

forward and walk in the power Jesus has given you access to.

Let's begin to wait with patience on the man who will lead us closer to Jesus!

Let's keep our clothes on and our legs closed!

Let's quit worrying about WHEN our man will come, and just TRUST God's timing!

Let's clean our mouths of all the filthy things we've allowed in!

Let's begin to believe who God says we are!

Let's make purity a priority!

Let's fall in love with JESUS!

Let's... joking. I'm done.

THE END

Thank you to the <u>Mamas of the Good Girl Gang</u> for making this book possible.

Melody Williams

Tina Tatum

Ann Sparks

Lynn Murley

Carmel Rich